Alabaster Boxes
A Woman's Heart Service to the Lord

By

Barbara Ellen Houston McCain

Copyright © 2019
Barbara Ellen Houston McCain
All rights reserved.
ISBN: 9781080182879
Also available on Kindle e-books

Mark 14:3-9
And being in Bethany in the house of Simon the leper, as he sat at meat,
there came a woman having an alabaster box of ointment of spikenard very precious;
and she brake the box, and poured it on his head.
And there were some that had indignation within themselves, and said,
Why was this waste of the ointment made?
For it might have been sold for more than three hundred pence, and have been given to the poor.
And they murmured against her.
And Jesus said, Let her alone; why trouble ye her? She hath wrought a good work on me.
For ye have the poor with you always, and whensoever ye will ye may do them good:
but me ye have not always.
She hath done what she could:
she is come aforehand to anoint my body to the burying.
Verily I say unto you,
Wheresoever this gospel shall be preached throughout the whole world,
this also that she hath done shall be spoken of for a memorial of her.

Introduction

What a joy and peace to my soul came as I thought on the words of Jesus concerning the woman with the alabaster box. He said of her, *She hath done what she could. Mark 14:8*

He was not only defending Mary from the criticisms of those in the room, but He was praising her in front of them all. In her heart, I believe she heard His words as a sweet balm to her soul. She must have thought: "He understands me. He knows why I did this." Wonderful Jesus. "Though others scorn and criticize, He gives blessing to my act. Oh, how I love Him." The tears that probably streamed down her face, were ones of love, honor, blessing and awe at what she understood He would do for her. He would die, He would carry her sins, her short comings, her faults. All that was to come, but in that present moment, it was as if He spoke the ultimate commendation to her soul, "Well done, my good and faithful servant." She had walked quietly into a room. But it was not just a room she had entered, she had also entered into the physical presence of her Lord. Remembering her actions and her faith, our souls can join the echo of: "Well done, Mary, well done."

The joy and peace I felt in mentally viewing this scene went much deeper than thinking about Mary. It began to dwell on that one phrase, *She hath done what she could.* A new thought penetrated my being: God does not require of us to do those things He has reserved for others. Each of us is to do that which we can. The Lord puts limits on us and He gives the opportunities. Rest my soul. "Do what you can" is a message to my often troubled heart. Out of love for Him, I desire to do so much more, as well I should. But rest, dear heart within, the Creator of all the earth formed you and constantly molds you. He knows what His desires and goals are for you. Others may sing with a beautiful voice, I will have to wait for Heaven. Yet still I can join in the chorus here below. Others can have that large number of children I dreamed about, but I can rejoice in the three I have. Through ministry, I can reach out to other little ones with the love of Jesus. Others could go to the foreign mission field, but my missionary vision was narrowed to the United States by illness. Yet I can be a witness here. Peace. Rest, my soul. Do what you can, even if it is just that moment in time when you break the Alabaster Box of your heart's devotion and pour it spiritually on His head and wipe the oil on His feet in your mind's commitment. Do what you can. Rest in Him, my soul.

Those are the lessons I carried in my heart for a month as I meditated on this passage and this particular phrase. *She hath done what she could.* Then the additional thoughts started to flow, the thoughts of this book. As we share this devotional journey together, may your souls be blessed, not by the words of my pen, but the words of our Savior as He speaks to your heart. May we each come before Him with tender hearts of love, ready to give of our devotion and praise. May we each rest in the assurance that God knows what we can do for Him. Let us reach for that goal, and also rest in the knowledge that to serve Him is the greatest honor we can ever have in this life. May we each hear our name added to the commendation, "Well done, my good and faithful servant."

Table of Contents

Chapter One
The things that we _MUST_ do - That which is required of us

She hath done what she could

This beautiful phrase from our theme verses, shows the heart of Mary in her love for Christ. Taken out of context and out of understanding of Scriptural doctrines, some might think that just to try to do whatever we think would be considered noteworthy and right, that it would be enough to please the requirements of the holy God. Many times, it is said of a person that she was such a nice person, she was always trying to be helpful, surely she has earned her way into Heaven. It is good to be kind. It is good to do that which is helpful, but those deeds are not what determine our eternal destiny. Indeed, our theme verses do not speak of salvation, but of service. We can only serve someone we know. Mary knew Jesus.

She knew that He was indeed the Son of God, the Savior, who would soon die for her sins. If the doing of her act that day, and the tenderness of her character, were enough to guarantee the blessing of eternity, Christ would not have had to die. Mary would not have needed a Savior. Mary had understood as she sat at His feet in teaching sessions that He was the One who had come to fulfill all the requirements of Messiah. He would set His people free, not from Roman rule, but from the rule of sin and death. Jesus had raised her brother Lazarus from the dead. Only God could do that. She knew that Jesus was the Christ, the Son of the Living God. Jesus had told His followers that He would go to Jerusalem and that there He would die. Very few had listened with hearts of understanding to realize that the time was near. Mary had listened. Mary had understood. The act that she was doing was as much a statement of her belief in His coming atoning death than if she had preached a sermon that day. She was serving Him who would die for her. She understood it was an act of love for the One who would make salvation available through His coming death. The needed atonement was to pay the price for salvation. That atonement for all can only come from the One who holds all in His hands.

Neither is there salvation in any other:
For there is none other name under heaven given among
men,
Whereby we must be saved.
Acts 4:12

The blessing of Mary's act, that would earn praise from the blessed Son of God, was not just for that moment of time. He said *Verily I say unto you, Wheresoever this gospel shall be preached throughout the whole world, this also that she hath done shall be spoken of for a memorial of her. Mark 14:9.* It was a memorial of her service, her love and her devotion. But it was not in reference to any act that would or could earn her salvation. In fact, the very act itself, the one of anointing her Savior for His coming death and burial, spoke volumes of her understanding of true salvation. That eternal salvation of her soul and of ours could only be purchased by the very One whom she anointed. It was Jesus who would die. It was Jesus who would be buried. And it was Jesus who would be the Redeemer! The memorial to Mary is that she understood this!

Mary's acknowledgment of Jesus as Lord and King, the anointed Priest and Savior, the One who was to die, is paramount for our understanding of the difference between salvation and service. We must also believe all the same things about Jesus that Mary did for salvation's work to be done in our hearts. We must by faith believe, not perform some physical act. In believing today, we have the advantage that He has already died, was already buried and has already risen again. Mary believed by faith in the coming events. But it is the same. In salvation it is required of us to believe in His atoning death, burial and resurrection. We must acknowledge Him. That is true salvation.

That if thou shalt confess with thy mouth the Lord Jesus,
and shalt believe in thine heart that God hath raised him from the
dead,
thou shalt be saved.
For with the heart man believeth unto righteousness;
And with the mouth confession is made unto salvation.
Romans 10:9-10

Despite the commendation given to Mary of her action, that she had done what she could, there are those things that are required for us (and for her) in the area of salvation. Those things are not simple deeds of love or elaborate ceremonies or long times of penitence. When Jesus cried from the Cross, "It is finished," He did not mean just the events of the day. He meant the eternal work of salvation was finished. All had been done was to provide the purchase price for our souls. Jesus has done it all and, truly, all to Him we owe! To understand that salvation is a gift purchased with the precious blood of Jesus should cause us each to fall on our knees and worship Him. There is a special consummation of eternal understanding that defines the difference between that which we must do for salvation and that which we can do in service. It takes all the striving and doubt away.

The knowledge of what we MUST do

The peace and rest in knowing that God blesses what "we can do" for Him does not dismiss the fact that He also has those things that are required of us. We do not serve a God who is weak or vacillating. He is not one that says, "Oh, it is okay, I will accept all actions, after all you probably have an excuse." He is not one to say, "I am a God with no rules, do as you will, in the end I will accept it."

He is a God of absolutes, a God of direction, a God of standards. What a wonder there is in that realization! We have a God who is truly Divine! He is to be our constant, our source of understanding of what is true and holy. Truly, there is none like unto Him! Because He is truly the One God, we can trust Him and His Holy Word.

Jesus said, *I am the way, the truth, and the life: John 14:3*

This verse illustrates the steadfastness of our God, the One we can follow, trust and receive eternal life from. It was no mindless matter that spawned us in eons past. It is the purposeful, all powerful Creator who formed us in His likeness and molds us still. As a loving Father, He gives clear cut requirements for us to be what we should and can be in His sight. Always, in His Word, He speaks these commands with the clarity that Jesus spoke when He told of the requirements of eternal life in the remainder of John 14:6, the part after the colon:

no man cometh unto the Father, but by me.

That is true salvation. That is the way and the truth and the life that we must believe in.

What is required of man before the Holy God?

The requirement of all men is for them to acknowledge God as God and Jesus as our Savior.

Read John 11:25-27, speaking of a conversation between Jesus and Mary's sister, Martha:

> *Jesus said unto her, I am the resurrection and the life:*
> *he that believeth in me, though he were dead; yet shall he live:*
> *And whosoever liveth and believeth in me shall never die.*
> *Believest thou this?*
> *She saith unto him, Yea, Lord: I believe that thou art the Christ,*
> *the Son of God, which should come into the world.*

What question did Jesus ask Martha?

What did He say was required of a person to believe about Him?

Read Genesis 1:1, Hebrews 11:3. Who alone gave and can give life?

Read John 3:36. What happens to a man who does not believe in the God of life?

It is required to believe in the One true God in order to share in His life. We must have faith in Him that He is God. Hebrews 11:6 speaks eloquently of this requirement:

But without faith it is impossible to please him [God]:
for he that cometh to God must believe that he is,
and that he is a rewarder of them that diligently seek him.

Why do you think it is impossible to please God unless we believe Him in faith?

What does it say about how you feel about a person, if you do not have faith in them?

Tell some of the reasons you have faith in God:

The word *"must"* in Hebrews 11:6, is a very strong word. In English, it means that we absolutely, positively have to do something. In Greek, the word means that something is necessary, especially in order that something else will occur.

What MUST we do in order to come to God?

What will God do for those that believe in Him?

What are some of those rewards?

So the first part of the first requirement of God is that we MUST believe that He is.

The second part of that requirement is that we MUST believe that Jesus is the Son of God, the only Savior.

Only by believing that Jesus is the Son of the living God can we have God's eternal life.

What three names did Martha say she believed belonged to Jesus in John 11:27?

Let's examine these names and how they relate to God's requirement of belief. Read the verses noted and comment on them:

Lord:
Acts 2:36

Romans 14:9

Luke 6:5

I Corinthians 8:4-6

Christ:
John 4:24-25

John 6:68-69

Ephesians 5:20

The Son of God:
John 3:35-36

John 3:18

Matthew 14:33

Matthew 1:1, 18

Romans 5:10

The first requirement of God is easily stated in the Bible:
We must believe in God and that Jesus Christ is His Son.

We could now say that the second requirement is like unto the first!
We must believe that Jesus died and paid the full price for our sins.

Tell the significance of the following verses:

Romans 10:9-13

Hebrews 10:10-12

Hebrews 10:16-20

Hebrews 13:20-21

Jesus summed all this up in one simple and powerful statement when He answered Nicodemus' questioning heart about how to obtain eternal life with God:

Marvel not that I say unto thee, Ye must be born again. John 3:7
The primary requirement of God is found in that verse:

Ye <u>MUST</u> be born again.

Before salvation's work of grace, we are all dead in our sins, bound for an eternal destiny without God. All that changes when we are born again. That spiritual birth is a one-time commitment of heart to the truth that we need the redemption that can only be found in Christ. It is when we truly believe on Him. We must be born again for our spiritual lives to be changed and our spiritual destiny with God assured. Jesus Christ paid the price for that change, that redemption, that salvation. Believing in Him delivers us into that miraculous change called being born again.

Oh, how Mary rejoiced to see the day when her redemption would be paid. Oh, how Mary's heart must have ached to know that Jesus, blessed Jesus, would demonstrate His love in so great a manner that He would die. For that truth, she came to anoint Him. For that truth, we must bow before Him in believing faith.

When I Survey the Wondrous Cross

When I survey the wondrous cross, On which the Prince of Glory died,
My richest gain I count but loss, And pour contempt on all my pride.
Forbid it, Lord! That I should boast, Save in the death of Christ my God:
All the vain things that charm me most, I sacrifice them to His blood.
See, from His head, His hands, His feet, Sorrow and love flow mingled down:
Did e'er such love and sorrow meet, Or thorns compose so rich a crown?
Were the whole realm of nature mine, That were a present far too small;
Love so amazing, so divine, Demands my soul, my life, my all.
Isaac Watts

****

The things we **<u>MUST</u>** do to meet the requirements of God are these:

1)   *Believe that God is.*

2)   *Believe that Jesus Christ is His Only Begotten Son.*

3)   *Believe that Jesus died for our sins, was buried and rose again.*

Through meeting these requirements, which are truly all wrapped up together, we will be cleansed of our sins, clothed in His righteousness, born again, saved eternally and made children of the Living God.

But as many as received him, to them gave he power to
become the sons of God,
even to them that believe on his name:
Which were born, not of blood, nor of the will of the flesh,
nor of the will of man but of God.
John 1:12-13
****

Thoughtful Questions:

1) Tell why you have confidence that the woman with the Alabaster Box believed that Jesus was the Christ, the Son of God.

2) Was it her actions or the belief in her heart that saved her?

3) What did she believe Jesus would do to save her?

4) How do you know this?

****

Quietly in her room, the woman stared at the beautiful box.
Alone it sat, on her wooden chest.
The light glimmered on its surface,
Reflecting its richness.
Softly she stepped closer, taking in its beauty.

The scent arose to meet her.
      Through invisible cracks in the seal,
      Speaking of the fragrance within.
Solemnly she remembered the words of her Lord.
      He would go to Jerusalem to die.
      For her sins He would perish,
      Securing her eternal salvation.
Decidedly she reached forth her hand in wonder and awe.
      All her belief was bound in the lifting of her heart and hand.
      He is Lord, He is Christ, He is my Savior.
      Doing this I will honor Him.
      Doing this I will anoint Him beforehand for His
burial,
      As He will surely die, As He said.
My heart is Yours, my faith is in You,
      take this my offering of what I believe.
Yea, Lord, I believe that Thou art the Christ,
      the Son of the Living God,
      Yea, Lord, I believe.

Chapter Two
Give of Your Best to the Master

What if someone asked us the question, "What is the best item in your home?" As we looked around our own home for the answer, each of us might pick something different. Some would immediately walk to the expensive antique heirloom passed down for generations and recently valued at an incredible sum. Some might walk into the kitchen and point to their modern appliance that makes life easier for them. Some might lovingly caress the well-polished surface of their long dreamed of baby grand piano. Some might laughingly walk directly back to their bedroom, plop down on the luxurious pillow top mattress and sigh with comfort. Others might thoughtfully pick up their favorite reference Bible. Others might pat the solid walls of the home itself. In American modern life, the answers would be varied about the thing we count "the best."

In Africa or the tropical jungles of Brazil, the answers might be very different. Maybe the best item would be the new plow, brought inside at night to protect it from thieves. Or maybe it would be the carefully woven hammock, or the sharp spear for killing game, or the netting that keeps the children safe from disease carrying mosquitos at night. In other lands, it might be the wood burning stove that keeps the home and its people from freezing in Northern climes, or the layers of warm and cherished handmade quilts.

Around the world and through all time, each person has valued something they own as "the best" to them.

The best that Mary had to give to the Savior that day long ago was an Alabaster Box and the oil that lay within. She knew its monetary value, she knew its significance and she knew its personal worth. All that it was, she took in her hands that day and gave of her best to the Master.

...there came a woman having an alabaster box of ointment of
spikenard very precious;
and she brake the box, and poured it on his head. Mark 14:3
Mary gave of her best, what is our best to give?

Giving our best:
> *What can I give Him?*
> > *The shepherd might have brought Him a lamb.*
> *What can I give Him?*
> > *The star shone its brightest rays on the manger.*
> *What can I give Him?*
> > *His mother prepared the finest of linen wraps,*
> > > *soft and warm.*
> *What can I give Him?*
> > *Joseph gave Him his best care and home.*
> *What can I give Him?*
> > *Mary gave Him ointment very precious.*
> *What can I give Him?*
> > *I'll give Him my heart and my life,*
> > > *my time and my talent,*
> > *I'll give Him my treasures and my family,*
> > > *my fears and my dreams.*
> > *But most of all,*
> > > *I'll give Him the best that I have.*

Throughout all the ages of time, man has been challenged to give of his best to the God who created Him. There is to be a "first and foremost" position for God in our hearts, minds, emotions and goals. If there is this priority of God awareness and devotion, our lives will be the best that they can be. The enemy of our souls constantly tries to tempt us to keep that "best" for ourselves. Yet in that keeping, we often find that we either lose what we considered best, or it tarnishes in its value. We must never fall for Satan's deception.

Let's go to the beginning of time and see how this principle applies:

And the LORD God formed man of the dust of the ground, and breathed into his nostrils the breath of life; and man became a living soul.
And the LORD God planted a garden eastward in Eden, and there he put the man whom he had formed.
And out of the ground made the LORD God to grow every tree that is pleasant to the sight, and good for food; the tree of life also in the midst of the garden, and the tree of knowledge of good and evil...........
And the LORD God took the man, and put him into the garden of Eden to dress it and to keep it. Genesis 2:7-9, 15

Why would God have planted a special Garden for Adam to live in?

Since all of the world had not yet been affected by sin, how do you think the Garden of Eden was different than other places?

What does the passage say about the quality of the trees and of the fruit?
     1) The trees were:

     2) The fruit was:

God gave Adam the best place to live, the best food for his body and the best job for his time. Because God knew what was best for the man, He also gave him one rule. Read Genesis 2:16-17. What was that one rule?

God not only provided the best for Adam's physical being, but He provided the best for his companionship. Read Genesis 2:18-25.

What need did God know Adam had, mentioned in verse 18?

How was the relationship between Adam and the animals good?

There is a great contrast in this passage between what was good for Adam and what was the best for him. Verse 20 tells why Adam needed the best in companionship. State what that need was:

Think deeply. Why should Woman meet the needs of Adam, the representative first man, and be the best for him?

Now read Genesis 3:1-6.

Do you remember what <u>all</u> the trees of the garden were like?

Do you remember what <u>all</u> the fruit was like?

What did the serpent make Eve see in that which was forbidden? (Verse 6)

The serpent deceived Eve into thinking that the fruit of the Tree of knowledge of good and evil was the "best" for her. But all around her, God had placed what was truly the very best for her and warned of the consequences of eating of the forbidden fruit. Even today, Satan works this way with people in deceiving them about what is best for their lives. Write down some of your thoughts on this matter.

To demonstrate the importance of choosing that which is God's best, let us compare some verses from the account of the Garden of Eden.

Compare how Adam and Eve felt in their hearts before the Fall and after the Fall:
Genesis 1:27-28a, 2:25:

Genesis 3:7-8

What was God's revealed plan for Man and Woman in The Garden of Eden:
Genesis 1:26-31

Genesis 3:16-19

Where could Adam and Eve dwell:
Genesis 2:7-15

Genesis 3:22-24

What commands did God give to Adam and Eve:
Genesis 1:28, 2:16-17

Genesis 3:16-19

What are your thoughts on the difference between living in the center of God's will and making choices that force you out of the area of blessing?

Is the trade worth it?

Read this precious verse describing God's desire for each of our lives and comment on it:

For I know the thoughts that I think toward you, saith the LORD,
thoughts of peace, and not of evil, to give you an expected end.
Jeremiah 29:11

How can we know God's thoughts and what is truly the best for us? The answer is so filled with simplicity that we should have an awe fill our souls: the way is to follow God's Word and heed His instructions. As we learned in Chapter One, God has not left us without instructions for living. The Lord has made available to us in Scripture all that we need in knowledge of His ways. To reinforce that knowledge, God has not left us comfortless but has sent the Holy Spirit to dwell within each believer to give direction and peace when we follow God's will. God states in Jeremiah 29:11 that He has always planned the best and given the best for us. We need to not only choose the best that He offers, but give of our best back to Him. The manner in which we give to God shows the condition of our hearts.

Read Genesis 4:1-5

When verse three describes the offering of Cain, what does it say?

Is the word "best" or "first" used to describe Cain's offering?

What word is used to describe Abel's offering?

God had respect unto the offering of Abel because he gave of the firstlings of his flock, the first and foremost. How did this show his respect for God?

How did this show his trust in God?

Read Genesis 4:6-12.

How did Cain's greed, anger and jealousy demonstrate his <u>lack</u> of putting God first in his life? What did Cain lose by not giving God the best in his offering?

Most people note that Abel gave a blood sacrifice to God, which is of course of primary importance. But did you ever before notice that he <u>also</u> gave of the <u>best</u>, the very best of the flock, while Cain is noted as just giving of the fruit of the land? Could it be possible Cain brought just a portion, though not necessarily the best of the fruits? How does this bring new meaning to you in this famous passage?

Read Genesis 22:1-2.

The words in verse two describe Abraham's evaluation of his son, Isaac. God said that he was Abraham's *only son Isaac, whom thou lovest.* The concept in the Hebrew for the phrase *whom thou lovest,* is the best and the much loved darling son. Abraham, indeed, did have another son, but Isaac was his firstborn of God's promise, the best that he had. What did God ask Abraham to do with his "best?"

A burnt offering is a type of a total giving: totally consumed, totally given to God. This is what God asked Abraham to do with Isaac, to give him totally to God. How did Abraham's response in verse three demonstrate Abraham's relationship to God?

Read Genesis 22:6-8.

Do you notice the important wording of Abraham's answer to Isaac's question of *where is the lamb for a burnt offering?* Abraham answered in verse 8, with great tenderness of heart, *My son, God will provide himself a lamb for a burnt offering.* Wonderful love of Abraham for his Friend, God! Abraham believed that God would provide a lamb for the offering on the top of the mountain that day! Further study also shows that Abraham trusted that God would do something miraculous as God's promises through Isaac would be kept. Also, in a way he could not perhaps fully understand, this journey of Abraham's faith up Mount Moriah, teaches us another lesson. It is the lesson of John 3:16:

> *For God so loved the world, that he gave his only begotten Son,*
> *so that whosoever believeth in him should not perish, but have*
> *everlasting life.*

How did God give His best, for us?

Examples of the Best Given
Read the following verses regarding giving of the best to others, and comment on the verses:

Genesis 43:11-12

Genesis 47:5-6

Exodus 22:5

Luke 15:22-24

When God gave His commandments regarding worship in the tabernacle, He often referred to the best of materials, of woven cloth, of exacting regulations. He also referred to the best in offerings. Why do you think God asked the people of Israel to bring of the best of their substance to the tabernacle as an offering to the Lord?

This same principle is noted in the dedicated offerings to go to the priests. Read Numbers 18:12-13, and note that the "first fruits of the first fruits" were to be given to the priests.

What does that say about our care for the pastors God has given to us?

In reviewing the laws regarding offerings, God again emphasizes that the people bring of the first fruits.

Read Leviticus 2:14. Why do you think it would be important to give of the first fruits to God?

Think of how this decision relates to:
Trust in God:

Honor for God:

Obedience to God:

Lessons taught to others (especially children) about our relationship to God:

Why would some people today be tempted <u>not</u> to give of their first fruits in the form of a tithe of their income?

What would that say about their faith?

****

God gave the **best** to us. We are to give the **best** to Him.

1)   Giving of the first fruits in our lives, in the form of tithes, special offerings, devotion, and priority, demonstrates our trust in and honor for God.

2)   Satan will tempt us to keep what we consider "the best" for ourselves, but if we do, it will often lose its value or corrupt our walk with God. Greed is the consuming desire to have what is best for ourselves in the wrong way. Greed corrupts, but honor enhances the value of what we have.

3)   God gave us the prime example of giving of "the best" when He gave His only begotten, much loved Son, Jesus Christ, on the Cross for our sins. The knowledge of this gift should bring devotion and love from our hearts to give of our "best" to God, who will bless the giving with His love.

Every good gift, and every perfect gift is from above, and cometh down from the Father of lights, with whom is no variableness, neither shadow of turning. James 1:17

****

Thoughtful Meditation and Questions:

When the woman brought the alabaster box to Jesus there were specific words to describe that which she brought. The alabaster must have gleamed with a shine that bespoke its worth. Ordinary vessels were made of clay or fired pottery. But this vessel was of finely carved and polished alabaster, a stone of great beauty and worth. The words used to describe the contents of spikenard oil are "very precious." In Greek, those words hold the meaning of "genuine and unadulterated, trustworthy, and of great value." The box was valuable, the contents even more valuable. The Book of John, Chapter 12, mentions that it was "very costly." They were the best that Mary had. Then it says that *she brake the box, and poured it on his head. Mark 14:3.* The word for break is one that means "to crush completely, to shatter to pieces with no recovery possible." The contents were totally poured out, running down Jesus' head, His body and onto His feet. All that was left was a lovely thick odor that filled the house. (John 12:3)

Mary knew that God would give His best, His precious Son, the Messiah, for her in death. It would be a "complete breaking," a complete pouring out of His blood and body. She desired to give of her best to the Master in just such a way, not counting the cost, because the cost of the alabaster and the ointment could not be compared with her love for Christ. She did not seek to save some for herself, or the box for the ornamentation of her chamber, she gave all of the best to Him.

1)   What do you think Mary might have thought as she made her decision to break the box?

2)   How did her action demonstrate the priority of her devotion to Jesus?

3)   Is there anything in your life that you count as a valuable treasure?

4)   Even though you might not have to break it or pour it all out, in what way could you give this treasure or use it to serve Christ?

5)   How would that affect the way you felt about your belongings?

****

"Jesus is coming," Simon had sent the message
to her beloved brother.
He would prepare for Him the best feast in all of Bethany.

Lazarus flushed with excitement, the Master was coming,
the One he owed his very life to.
He would bring the best of his wine for the feast.

Martha scurried about, Christ was on His way as they spoke,
The Christ who was the Resurrection and the Life.
She would bake her best bread and help with the serving.

What can I give Him? thought Mary in her heart.
I have no better feast or wine or bread,
I can offer nothing of the works of my hands,
What can I give?

In her room that night, Mary must have prayed,
Lord, what can I give to Him?
> *I want to give Him the best I have.*
> *Her eyes opened to see the alabaster box,*
>> *the one her father perhaps had given her,*
>> *the one to be saved perhaps for her dowry,*
>> *the one to be used for precious things.*
> *All these years it had sat in her chamber.*

He is precious, my heart belongs to Him,
He is to be the bridegroom of my soul.
> *Then she knew.*
Her best was the box and its costly oil.
> *But did she know,*
> *The best was truly the act of her love,*
>> *poured out on Him?*

Chapter Three
Give of Your Concern for the Reactions of Others to God

Mary did not do her act of devotion in private. She broke the Alabaster Box and poured out its ointment in front of a room full of people, probably mostly men. Nothing was hidden, the act was seen by all those gathered at the feast. Her brother Lazarus was there, as was their friend Simon the leper. Jesus' disciples were there and perhaps more invited guests. Did Mary hesitate at the doorway before she entered? Whatever her feelings were at the moment, her focus was clear. That focus made all else fade away. There was only One in the room that mattered. There was only One who would die for her sins. There was only One upon whom she would pour the gift within the Alabaster Box. The Scripture does not mention that Mary uttered even one word. Never in the recorded encounter does she try to explain her act. Jesus knew, He knew! In her heart, Mary knew the worshipful intentions that urged her on. The reactions of others did not stop her as she continued her actions even while some in the room objected. The reactions did not matter, because all that filled her mind was the presence of Jesus and her understanding of what He would do for her. It is what He would do for the others, too.

Yet, that room full of people might have distracted some.

All through our lives, we will find that our thoughts about how others view us will be real. Sometimes, these thoughts are for good. How we communicate our love to someone else is important. How we should be dressed for a certain occasion should not be dependent upon our whims, but on what is appropriate so that we do not bring a negative reaction on those we might want to witness to of our salvation in Christ. How we act in a public meeting ruled by set standards of conduct, such as a court room, is important, not only for our testimony, but even for our safety! Disruptors are often sentenced to contempt of court and a day in jail! Rules of conduct are not always to be shunned or defied. They give us a standard of right perimeters for behavior, ones that will bring honor to our own character and that of our Savior. In those cases, what could be called "peer pressure" is helpful.

But, most of the time, we think of "peer pressure" in a negative manner. Many a child has taken a dare because of their fear of what others would think of them if they refused. It might even be a dare that would cause them harm and the action of which would never have been considered if they had been alone. One of the lessons mothers hope to teach their children is that the dares of "peer pressure" do not have to be taken.

Many a young person or teen has failed to turn away or climb back down from the level of temptation to please others. Sometimes it has proven to be to their ruin. Peer pressure has caused even the normally shy person to want to prove themselves to others and take that first drug, or cigarette, or drink of alcohol. It has caused many a child to do the naughty deed, steal a dollar from their mother's purse, or act up in the classroom. Peer pressure, even if just from one or two others, can be very dangerous. Have you ever seen a mob in action? Many in that group are just reacting to the fear of not fitting in, not doing what others expect them to do. How very like the actions of Satan in our lives. He will often try to push us to do what we would not otherwise have done. True bravery is often turning away, as if we were in a mob, and walking out the back side to get help. Oh, how mighty and powerful the push of others can be to do wrong.

Then there is the peer pressure that comes silently within our minds. There is that whisper, "What will others think of me if I say or do this?" Many a witness for Jesus has been delayed because of those whispers. Being afraid of being accepted is a reality. Often if we feel the godly urge to do that which is right, the whisper will come. Many brave and righteous actions or speeches have not happened because of that little whisper. Perhaps, the most powerful hindrance of peer pressure is found in the whispered thought that no one else hears. The hand is stayed from the act of good, the words are swallowed back from a witness, the answer of bravery goes undone. All because of the fear of what others would think.

Apply this principle to an understanding of James 4:17: *Therefore to him that knoweth to do good, and doeth it not, to him it is sin.*

Think of Mary at the threshold of the entry into the area of the feast. What forms of peer pressure might have kept her from entering and doing her act of devotion?

Even in the performance of that which would be a memorial of faith for her life, Mary had to face the conventions of the day. Though women were honored in Jewish life, concerning behavior there were still some rules of conduct to be observed. In the Temple there was the Court of the Women. This was sometimes called the Middle Court, located between the Court of the Gentiles and the Court of the Men. Our modern sensitivities might seem to object to these divisions, but think of the honor in the creation of this special Court for Women. In some of the surrounding cultures to Israel of that day in history, women were excluded from public worship. Yet in the Temple of Jerusalem, there was a special court for them to enter. God knew the hearts of all His people: man, woman, child and even foreigners that loved Him. He allowed a place for each and for all.

At the feast of Simon the leper, there would have been customary forms of conduct. The men would have entered into the dining area and the women might have served. It would have been men only at the feast. The women would eat in the kitchen or elsewhere of the same food, but the feast was reserved for the men and Jesus. Mary would have known her expected position. And then there was Mary herself. In Scripture, she appears reserved, perhaps a very modest and quiet woman. When she entered the room that evening, she had to know others would be surprised, but her love and dedication supported her walk from the doorway to Jesus' place at the feast. The looks of the others were not what concerned her, it was only what she had to do for Jesus that mattered. Mary did not let "peer pressure" stop her from her task. It did not make her turn back or still her hand in the pouring of the oil.

Perhaps no one is free from the feelings of peer pressure. So often we limit it to the trials of the teenage years. However, the mere fact of advertising on television attests to the fact that our standing with the opinions of others has great influence. Sales of certain products will soar when it is known that the majority of women over 50 are purchasing it. Husbands spend many dollars every Valentine's Day, often to ensure that they are doing that which is expected and accepted in modern times. Conversely, a soldier on the field of battle will often persevere knowing what others around him would think if he were to run away. Peer pressure is not always negative. Often the ideals and emotions of others will influence us for good. But there are times it has the opposite effect, causing someone to follow the wrong way so as not to appear different.

We must give our feelings concerning "peer pressure" to the Lord. Our actions and thoughts must be based upon what God desires, not upon what those around us would try to dictate.

Let us view the scene of our Scripture passage to see how others reacted to Mary that day.

And being in Bethany in the house of Simon the leper, as he sat at meat,
there came a woman having an alabaster box of ointment of spikenard very precious;
and she brake the box, and poured it on his head.
And there were some that had indignation within themselves,

and said, Why was this waste of the ointment made?
Mark 14:3-4

We have thought of Mary and her act of devotion. Now let us look at the others at the feast that saw what she did. The most obvious reaction by those watching is found in the statement: *And there were some that had indignation within themselves. Mark 14:4.* Three words stood out to me from this sentence:

Some: Some means "not all!" How often we think that the reactions of the "some" ones in our lives have the most influence. There will always be those "some-ones" who object to your stand for Christ, those "some-ones" who will not understand your motivations, those "some-ones" who are quick to judge. The Scripture does not tell us how many made up the "some." Perhaps even at the feasting place with Jesus, there were more that did not object. We know that Jesus did not, which we will study later. Consider these questions regarding the "some."

How can a small group influence the behavior and reactions of others?

Why are we as human vessels often influenced by the opinions of others that oppose us?

What should our reactions be to these objectors?

What does it appear Mary's reaction was to them?

Indignation: The dictionary defines the word indignation as "Displeasure at what seems unworthy or base; anger, mingled with contempt, disgust or abhorrence; righteous scorn." Displeasure may seem like a light word, but the words anger, contempt, disgust and abhorrence are words of great weight. These "some" were disgusted with Mary's actions! They expressed feelings of anger and contempt. What they thought was righteous scorn was truly an unrighteous feeling of angry judgment. Indignation often flows out of very self- centered thoughts. Look up the following verses and comment on them:

Romans 14:13:

Matthew 7:3-4:

I Timothy 6:4:

Romans 2:1:

Having read the entire passage in Mark 14:3-11, state some of the "self" reasons that the objectors might have had:

Within:

Where did the negative feelings start in these "some?" The started "within." This sadly says a lot about those that did not honor Mary's actions. They did not have spiritual understanding. While Mary had listened, not only with her ears, but with her heart, she had understood that Jesus would soon die for her sins. The "some" had most assuredly heard the same words from Jesus, but they had not truly listened to gain understanding.

In Proverbs 18:2, there are some very strong words about such a person. Comment on them:

Do you think these men thought themselves fools?

Job understood the importance of the thoughts of the heart. Read his prayerful thoughts concerning God in Job 31:4-7 and comment on them:

Read the following verses and relate to being of spiritual understanding:
Proverbs 4:23

Ecclesiastes 7:25a

Matthew 12:35

Matthew 15:18-19

There is a marvelous godly contrast concerning the heart in the following two verses:

Luke 6:45:   Comment on the difference between good treasures and evil treasures of the heart:

Ezekiel 11:19-20:   What is the answer on how to have a good treasured heart?

The objectors labeled Mary's pouring out of the ointment as "wasteful," yet it was an ointment to be used most probably for the burial of a loved one. Is there anyone that could deserve our love more than Jesus? What have we poured out for Him today? Is it a portion of our time, our money, our labor? Might others think that this is a waste? How would you answer them?

In Mark 14:5, the "some" state that the precious ointment and the alabaster box might have been sold for a good price and the money given to the poor. While it is good to help the poor, Christ is to be our primary object of affection. Often in serving Him, we will be led to help others. But any deed done outside of total devotion to Christ is empty indeed. That their objection was not out of pure hearts is shown by the ending sentence of Mark 14:5: *And they murmured against her.* The phrase *murmured against* is never used in a positive way in the Scripture. It means literally "to snort with anger!" What a vivid word. It also contains the idea of to threaten sternly and admonish. Most often it is shown as being done behind someone's back. When the Israelites murmured in the wilderness, the unity of the whole nation was affected and judgment often came. In the New Testament, Paul warns against murmuring, calling to the reader's mind the consequences of this Israelite history. In I Corinthians 10:1-11, he admonishes: *Moreover, brethren, I would not that ye should be ignorant, how that all our fathers were under the cloud, and all passed through the sea, ...But with many of them God was not well pleased: ... Neither let us tempt Christ, as some of them also tempted... Neither murmur ye, as some of them also murmured and were destroyed of the destroyer. Now all these things happened unto them for ensamples: and they were written for our admonition..."* When the Israelites murmured in the wilderness, they were actually murmuring against God. No matter whether they thought the criticism was against a person or a situation, all was under the hand of God. It was still the same in Simon the leper's house that day. Those in the house with Jesus were murmuring right in front of Him! God is present in all our times today, but how often do Christians "murmur" privately? Remember this attitude is always negative, never positive!

Lord,
Guard my lips in what they say.
Fill my mind with thoughts of Your grace.
Help me not to murmur against others,
Or against what You allow into my life,
For truly it is against You that I would complain.
Fill my heart with love and thankfulness
Constantly to You.

How could knowledge of the murmuring of others against something we have said or done affect us?

Does it trouble you when others do not understand your motivations in a matter?

Do you feel you have to explain yourself to them? How could this be negative? How could this be positive?

How could you apply the following verse in this case? *But sanctify the Lord God in your hearts: and be ready always to give an answer to every man that asketh you a reason of the hope that is in you with meekness and fear: I Peter 3:15.*

What are the two words in the verse that give a warning about our attitude when answering others?

In Mary's case, Jesus gave the answers for her. What a wonderful Savior we have! He is truly our Defender and Shield! Mark 14:6 states: *And Jesus said, Let her alone; why trouble ye her?...* To be troubled by the others means that they had meant to bring her grief, sorrow and weariness of soul. Have you ever been there? Did you plan to do something to bring God praise and others mocked you? Or perhaps they thought it was not of the quality desired and let you know, even in front of others? That is why it is so important that Mary had her focus clear! She knew Who she was seeking to serve and honor. It was not for the praise of others, it was only to do that which was laid on her heart as a praise offering to Christ. It is so important that we do all our service with that in mind. It is Christ alone who is to receive the praise. It is Christ alone to whom we are to pour out our offerings of honor.

Jesus finishes His sentence to those murmuring and adds: *she hath wrought a good work on me.* Even if all others in the room had criticized, Jesus gave honor to her act. It was a "good work" and she wrought it, completed it wholly, unto the Lord. The Greek wording gives the concept of the fact that Mary had fulfilled her ordained purpose! God had ordained it for her to do!

What was necessary for Mary to know God's ordained purpose in this act?

Even though God had ordained the work, who does Jesus praise?

What do you think He praised Mary for?

How could we apply the phrase "Faithfulness to obey" to Mary's actions?

Read Mark 14:7-9. How did Jesus answer the complainers?
    In verse seven:

    In verse eight:

    In verse nine:

There were perhaps many things that Mary could not have done that day, but this one thing she could do! And *she hath done what she could.* Oh, that at the end of each day, we could lay our heads down on our pillows and know that we have done what we could. What sweet peace must have flooded Mary's heart, what warm tears must have come to her eyes as she heard Jesus say these words of commendation! From the murmuring of others, to the praise of the Master! It is almost as if a scared glow suddenly fills the room. I am convinced that no others saw it, but Mary did. The Master has understood and it was enough. That should be enough for us through trials and taunting of others. It is enough that Jesus understands!

Jesus mentions that what she did that day *shall be spoken of for a memorial of her. Mark 14:9.* Part of the ministry of a memorial is to inspire others, as well as to remember an act or person. How does this deed of Mary inspire you?

No matter how many are around us, we are still individuals and are directly responsible to God. I had a child say to me once, "Being a Christian sometimes makes me feel so different and I am not sure I like that." My answer? "Yes, you are different and that is not bad. God says that you are a peculiar person! But in the Bible the word peculiar does not mean weirdly different, it is a badge of God's love and honor. In both Hebrew and Greek, the word peculiar means a personal possession of value. Always remember that you are different because you are a personal possession of God of great value to Him!"

How does this descriptive meaning of the word "peculiar" found in Exodus 19:5, Deuteronomy 14:2, Titus 2:14, and I Peter 2:9, make you feel about your ability to stand against negative peer pressure?

How could it be a danger to never think of yourself as different from the world?

There seems to have been two reactions to Jesus' words that day by those in the feast. It would appear that many of the "others" were deeply affected, even into silence, by the actions of Mary and the explanation by Jesus. Perhaps some were ashamed. Perhaps some called to remembrance the words Jesus had spoken concerning His impending death. Perhaps others pondered all those things in their hearts, marveling at Jesus' words of praise for Mary. I can almost see Lazarus fixing his eyes on his younger sister and having his heart fill with pride. As a single woman, she would have been his responsibility. She was not like Martha, nor did she need to be, as Martha was not like her. Martha had recognized Jesus as the Messiah and Lord, and so had Mary. They evidenced it in different ways, yet Lazarus could know that indeed they were of the followers of the

Christ, the Son of the Living God. That was the most important completion of his responsibility to his sisters. They would dwell with him in that eternal Glory forever. He, too, had done what he could.

Then there is Judas Iscariot. It appears that this transaction was the "tipping point" for him. Read Mark 14:10-11. He went out immediately to the chief priest to betray Jesus. What a strong word *betray* is. Judas knew in his actions that he was turning Jesus over to the enemies. Those enemies were *glad*. Knowing the thoughts of their plans against Jesus, their gladness is most evil indeed. They wanted to destroy Jesus, to kill Him, and they were rejoicing over the part of the plan that would make that happen. Judas was given money for his deed. How very shallow compared to the praise given to Mary as a memorial to her for all generations. His deed would memorialize his name as the betrayer of the precious Son of God. He set out to determine how he might *conveniently* betray Jesus. How sad that word *conveniently* is. In modern day life, many seek to do things in a convenient way, an easy way, an opportune way.

Serving Christ is never to be convenient to us. List some ways that you realize this is true in demonstrating how Christian service often times goes outside the norm, outside the easy way:

Read Joshua 24:15, and comment on how Joshua's statement is a good illustration of having godly commitment, no matter what others may do.

****

Mary molded her fingers around the box of alabaster.
Inside that glowing vessel was precious ointment,
The box was a thing of beauty in itself.
Long stored in her room,

Many times gazed upon.
It was filled to the full, it was precious indeed.
The world might have seen its value in money,
Friends might have expected her to use it after a death,
But Mary knew in her heart,
It was only of value if it could be poured out,
On Him who was most precious indeed.

The entry into the place of feasting was done quietly,
On soft feet she walked,
One step after the other,
Closer to Jesus.
Some seemed to be startled,
Some even rose from their seats as if to stop her.
Embarrass the guest of honor at the feast?
What did this woman think she was doing?
Taunts and sneers started to sound all around,
Her ears were attuned to their criticism,
But she did not stop.

With one swift movement of her hand, the seal was broken on the
vessel.
With one graceful lifting of her fingers, the ointment began to pour
out.
The angry sounds faded away and all that she heard,
Was the gentle sound of the oil,
Anointing His head,
Running down His face and hair,
Coating His garments and the skin beneath.
The job was done.
The oil was spent.
The box was empty,
Except for the fragrance, the fragrance that spoke of her love for her
Lord.

The voices rose again, the complaints were renewed,
But then came the only voice she desired to hear that day,
Jesus, Blessed Holy Jesus.
The words He spoke silenced all the others.
They were a comfort to her soul,
A lifting up of her spirit,
An assurance of hope.
"Yea, Lord, I have done what I could,"
Came the whisper from her heart.

Quiet feet took her back out of the room,
But the fragrance remained.

Chapter Four
Give of Your Destiny to the Lord

*And being in Bethany in the house of Simon the leper, as he [Jesus]
sat at meat,
there came a woman having an alabaster box of ointment of
spikenard very precious ... Mark 14:3*

As Mary held the alabaster box, she took her destiny in her
hands. If the box and ointment were part of her dowry, she would
spend it all. If it was to be her security for times of trial, she would
pour it all out. If it was to be used to anoint a loved one for burial, it
would be used on her most loved One. Her destiny was not of the
temporal or earthly, it was to be of the spiritual, eternal. She had
listened, she had understood, and she would honor Jesus in the best
way she could.

It took courage to walk into the room and perform the act.
For Mary, this may have been much more than we can understand.
She seems to have sat quietly at Jesus' feet when He taught at her
house. She had not answered back when she was rebuked by Martha
or praised by Jesus. When Lazarus died, she was not one at the tomb
lamenting, she was quietly in the house. Jesus told Martha to go tell
her sister that the Master called for her. Mary responded to His call,
came out of the solitude of that house, and Jesus talked with her. We
do not know all that He said to her gentle heart, but it was enough for
her to step to the tomb and see the miracle of Lazarus being raised
from the dead. Even in the breaking of the alabaster box, her blessed
act of honor, she seems not to speak a word. She has left all in Jesus'
care. Even the enablement to pour out the oil and do that one act of
faith would have required total trust. What she did that day will
forever be remembered as her destiny. She perhaps did not think at
all of her own honor or destiny. She wanted only to honor Christ.
She trusted Jesus to understand what she would do.

It was her destiny. It was what she understood as her step of faith. If that was ALL that she ever did in life, she did what she could. She placed her entire destiny in Christ's hands, eternal and temporal, even to that specific day when this brave act happened. Think of the consequences. She could have been made to "go to her room" in disgrace and sorrow over the misunderstanding of her deed. Others would surely rebuke her, but it did not matter. She knew her heart and she knew her Lord. She was to anoint Him before hand for His burial, knowing that in His death and resurrection He would secure her eternal destiny. In that simple, yet profound act, she proclaimed her belief in what Jesus had said in His teachings. She formed her belief as she sat at His feet, when many others had not truly listened enough to understand.

Mary knew she must trust Christ with the destiny of that day. We read of it in Mark 14. Mary came to anoint Jesus because she believed His words. She knew who He was and what He had come to do. She trusted the eternal Son of God and knew that her times and her destiny were in His hands.

My times are in thy hand: ... Make thy face to shine upon thy servant ... Psalm34:15-16

Be of good courage, and he shall strengthen your heart, all ye that hope in the LORD. Psalm 34:24

****

Examples of Trust in God for Their Destiny

Abraham:

Read Genesis 12:1-4

Abraham had to trust God in each step of his revealed destiny, but also by faith, he had to trust in that which he did not see.

He trusted God when he left his home in Ur to travel to a land he did not know. He trusted God to give him a son when he was in his old age. He trusted God to keep all the promises He had made, even when the way was not clear. Paul cites why the example of Abraham's life is so important in this area of trusting God for our temporal and eternal destiny:

He staggered not at the promise of God through unbelief;
but was strong in faith, giving glory to God;
And being fully persuaded that, what he had promised, he was able
also to perform. Romans 4:20-21

Tell how these words of the above verse can relate to your life:
    1)   "Staggered not"

    2)   "Unbelief"

    3)   "Strong in faith"

    4)   "Fully persuaded"

Joseph:

Read Genesis 37:5-11
1)   Do you think young Joseph fully understood the visions God gave to him of his future?

2)   What positive character "seeds" could have been planted in Joseph's mind because of the visions?

3)   We know Joseph chose the "good seeds" of excellence in character, but what temptations or "bad seed" thoughts might Satan have desired he follow as a result of the visions?

4)   Do you think a glimpse of our own destinies would help to mold our character, or destroy it?

5)   It is interesting that Joseph's brothers, who at this point of life represent the unspiritual of the world, could not understand his vision. The vision was of God and could have blessed them all if they had rejoiced in God's choosing of Joseph. But instead, what were the brothers' reactions?

Read Genesis 37:13-20
6)   What do you notice about the development of young Joseph's character in this account? (Hints: in obedience to his father, in diligence)

7)   Did you notice what the brothers called Joseph in verse 19? What was that title and how does it help you to know they did not understand God's purposes?

Read Genesis 37:21-28.
8)   What unique circumstances did God use to protect Joseph's life at this point?

9) How does this demonstrate that God had a unique purpose for Joseph's life and what God has planned will be done?

Joseph goes through many years of being faithful to God; in slavery, in imprisonment and in a foreign land. You can read of this passage of time and the exciting events in Genesis 37:36, 39:1–40:57.

10) List some of the reasons Joseph could have become bitter during this time:

11) Does he ever express bitterness?

12) What are some of the positive godly characteristics that Potiphar, the chief jailor, the fellow prisoners, and then Pharaoh saw in Joseph?

13) How did that affect their treatment of and confidence in Joseph?

Read Genesis 42:1-8, 45:1-15

14) The time had changed Joseph's brothers, and it had changed Joseph's position. Explain how you know that Joseph understood God's destiny for his life:

15) How do you think the brothers felt in realizing what God had done to save their lives?

16) Read Genesis 45:4-7 again. Notice what grace and spiritual understanding Joseph had of God's dealings in his life! There is still no bitterness demonstrated at all toward his brothers, no revenge sought or pride in his position boasted of. Instead there is joy!

17) Can you think of some situation in your own life that prepared you to be used of God to perform your purpose in service for God?

18) How can this account of Joseph in the Bible encourage you in your own life situations right now?

19) How could bitterness interfere with God's blessed choices for your life?

****

Oh Lord,
Help me, help us, to always choose trust in You instead of choosing bitterness or anger.
Help me, help us, to realize that each step on our journey of life is leading us deeper and deeper into Your perfect design.
Help me, help us, to lay at Your feet anything that would hinder praise and grace being demonstrated in our lives.
Oh Lord, help me, help us, never to forget the testimony of Joseph to our own lives.
Help me, help us, to always choose You.
****

David:

Read I Samuel 16:5-13

In the Bible there was another "younger brother," named David, who was chosen for leadership over his seven older brothers.

1)   What was the factor of God's choice of a future king, noted in verse seven?

2)   Who did Samuel choose to be with David when he was anointed?

God planned for David's brothers to be among his most loyal helpers when he came into prominence in Israel. Even though they criticized him when he went against Goliath, after the victory that day, they seemed to realize God's hand on their youngest brother's life. From then on their destinies were tied to David's. When David had to flee to the wilderness, all his brothers went with him. They stayed with him in adversity. When David became king, they were made captains and rulers *for every matter pertaining to God, and affairs of the king. I Chronicles 26:32.* What a blessing it must have been to them to see their own "little" brother promoted to king. What a blessing it must have been to David to have his brothers by his side in trial and in triumph!

1)   Is there anyone in your life that needs your rejoicing support in what God has chosen for their life?

2)   Is there anyone of whom you have been envious or bitter because they have been promoted above you?

3) How could recognition of God's choice for each individual's destiny help your attitudes?

Paul:

Read Acts 7:54-60, Acts 8:1

The Apostle Paul is perhaps one of the most surprising choices for leadership in the New Testament church. His name was originally Saul.

1) Who was consenting unto Stephen's martyrdom for Christ?

2) What interesting prayer did Stephen have for Saul in verse 60?

Read Acts 9:1-2

3) What were Saul's attitudes and actions toward Christians, called "the disciples of the Lord"?

Read Acts 9:3-6

4) What was Saul's attitude when God called to him?

5) Do you think Saul realized God was changing his life?

Read Acts 9:10-14

6)   What was Ananias' reaction to God calling him to minister to Saul. How did this affect Saul's destiny?

Read Acts 9:15-16

7)   What was God's title for Saul found in verse 15?

8)   How does that remind you of Joseph and David?

9)   How do you think Ananias felt when he heard God's words regarding Saul?

Read Acts 9:17-20

10)   What was the change in Ananias when he realized Saul's godly destiny?

11)   What title did Ananias give to Saul in verse 17?

How very special that Ananias entered into a total brotherly bond with Saul. Even though we do not hear more of Ananias, it seems logical that he remained a close defender and ally of Saul for the rest of his life. In fact, if we read Acts 9:21-25, we can imagine Ananias giving testimony to the other Christians of God's call on Saul's life.

Read Acts 9:25. Because the disciples, including Ananias, believed so much in Saul's destiny, they risked their own lives and protected him. Without the "entering in" of others to the call of God on Saul's life, we might not have the great testimony of his writings in the New Testament.

Read Acts 9:26-31

12)   Tell how these words let you know Saul was brave and consistent in his commitment to God's call on his life: "Assayed to join":

"Boldly":

"Preached":

Read Ephesians 3:7-12

13)   How did Paul feel about this future that God had given to him?

****

...for I believe God, that it shall be even as it was told me. Acts 27:25

Being confident of this very thing, that he which hath begun a good work in you will perform it until the day of Jesus Christ. Philippians 1:6
****

Thoughtful Meditation and Questions

Like Mary that evening at Simon's house, Paul had boldness and confidence in the Lord.

1)   How was her boldness different than Paul's?

2)   Do we have to be preachers like Paul, or to risk death, to show boldness and confidence in God's call on our lives?

3)   How might you demonstrate boldness and confidence in the destiny God has called you to?

4)   In what ways can you teach your children or others to be willing to confidently follow God's call on their lives?

5)   Describe how total trust in God relates to confidently following a vision of your destiny:

6)   What ultimate part of Mary's destiny was she confidently trusting Jesus for, that was demonstrated by her knowledge of His impending death and burial?

****

Mary stared at the box in her hands.
    The flicker of the oil lamps
        reflected in a thousand gleaming points of light
          from its surface.
    The gentle breeze from the open windows
      carried the soft scent ahead of her
        as she began to walk.
Step by step she came,
    one foot in front of the other,

softly, gracefully,
her gown swirling above her feet.
Step by step she came
through the doorway
into the hall.
Each step took her closer to Jesus.

"I listened to Him and I know,"
she thought.
"He said I had chosen that good part
when I sat at His feet.
But the best part for me
was what He said that day.
He is the Messiah.
He is the Resurrection and the Life.

He is my Resurrection.
He is my life.
He is my destiny.

Chapter Five
Give of Your Devotion

*And it came to pass, as they went, that he entered into a certain village
and a certain woman named Martha received him into her house.
And she had a sister called Mary, which also sat at Jesus feet, and heard his word.
But Martha was cumbered about much serving, and came to him, and said,
Lord, dost thou not care that my sister hath left me to serve alone? Bid her therefore that she help me.
And Jesus answered and said unto her,
Martha, Martha, thou art careful and troubled about many things: But one thing is needful:
And Mary hath chosen that good part, which shall not be taken away from her.
Luke 10:38-41*

*And being in Bethany in the house of Simon the leper, as he sat at meat,
There came a woman having an alabaster box of ointment very precious;
and she break the box, and poured it on his head.
... And they murmured against her.
And Jesus said, Let her alone: why trouble ye her? She hath wrought a good work on me.
Mark 14:3-6*

This chapter is on giving God our devotion. What a clearer understanding of devotion could there be than that of the spiritual picture of sitting at Jesus' feet, just listening and believing, just basking in the wonder of Who He really is, just praying that you have understood what He is speaking to your heart. What Mary did physically, we are called upon to do spiritually. In the lesson of devotion to God, we are invited to sit with Mary at the feet of Jesus, listening to Him as He speaks to our hearts. That time of listening led Mary to her act of devotion the day of the feast at Simon the leper's home. The breaking of the alabaster box and pouring of its contents was an act of devotion to her Lord, an acknowledgement of her love for Him. We too are invited to pour out our love and devotion to Jesus, knowing Him in our hearts.

It seems Mary of Bethany always chose the "better part" in her relationship to Christ. On the day she sat at His feet and on the day of the feast, her devotion and focus were only on Christ. It did not matter what the others said, her spiritual ears were tuned to His words. Part of her devotion was contained in that focus. All around must have faded from her priorities. It was Christ and only Christ that occupied her mind.

Have you often noticed the "intrusion" of other thoughts when you attempt to sit at the feet of Jesus in your devotions?

Note some ways this has happened in your life:

Can you think of practical ways to protect your mind from these intrusions and wanderings:

Think of Mary on that day in Luke 10:
What could have distracted her from sitting in the room listening to Jesus?

What decisions did she have to make in order to be there?

Discuss Martha's complaint and whether or not there is validity to it?

How could Mary have communicated with Martha before going into the room to listen to Jesus that might have helped the situation?

Could there have been a way on the part of either Martha or Mary to make this a better situation?

There must have been a great burden of desire to hear the teaching of Jesus that day that overrode all else in Mary's life. It is possible that because she sat at His feet so quietly that she was one of the few that truly understood His teaching. It is good for us to remember that Jesus was consistently preparing His followers for His death. He had clearly proclaimed what He was to do in Jerusalem. The prophecies of the Old Testament had fully proclaimed it. The hearts and minds of His followers should have been ready to understand and to receive His words. Yet it seems that few had truly listened and understood as evidenced by their reactions to the actual events. Mary's devotional life must have included meditating on Jesus' spoken words which she had hidden in her heart while sitting at His feet as He taught, and also the Old Testament scriptures she studied. Perhaps, as a woman in those days, she would have to listen as her brother shared with the other men at the house what he had gained at the synagogue. Perhaps this practice had prepared her to enter into the room of teaching that day. Continually hiding God's

Word, written and spoken, in her heart allowed her to think deeply on it, meditate on it, and apply it to her life each day. There had to be that kind of devotion in her heart and mind for her to have realized above almost all the others that Jesus had come to die for her as the Messiah of soul deliverance, not the worldly champion that Judas Iscariot perhaps wanted to make Him, or the good companion and mighty teacher that others saw, or even the leader of a religious movement. Mary of Bethany had understood, perhaps because of her great devotion, that Jesus was the Christ, the Son of the Living God, and that He would die for her sins and that of the world. It only made her love for Him richer.

How do you think a deep devotional life can help you to know God Himself in a deeper way?

How do you think a deep devotional life can help you to know yourself more clearly?

How do you think a deep devotional life can help you in your interactions with others?

We are truly blessed that as women in America we can hold the Word of God in our own hands. We can view the purpose of Christ, the intent of His way and the end results for ourselves. How much easier that should make it for us to be women of great devotion. Oh, the blessed grace of our Lord, let us never neglect it! Don't let the "cares" of this world, steal away the joy and peace of a devotional life. It is that very time of quiet devotion that will make the cares of our lives fall into perspective. It is that devotional time spent at His feet that will give us the grace, courage and strength to live for Him.

Think about how that devotional life affected Mary's actions of Mark 14. She must have prayed about how she could honor Christ, how she could give of herself wholeheartedly to Him. She must have thought deeply about it. What she did that night was a deliberate, conscience act. Perhaps she had stood outside the doorway with the alabaster box in hand waiting for just the right moment.

Let's think about that in our own lives:
    What are your "right moments" with Him?

Contrast that to Judas' thoughts of choosing a convenient time to betray Christ:

How would you state that Mary was fully worshiping Jesus with her act?

How would you state that Judas was fully departing from worship of Jesus with his act?

Read John 12:1-8. This is a description of the same incident. Did you learn anything new from this account?

Have you ever thought of where Mary was as she wiped Jesus' feet with her long hair? She was most probably on her knees, a very humbling position for a woman of wealth as she was. It was a very humbling position for a single woman to assume. Clearly, it was a demonstration of her total devotion to Christ, of honoring Him and recognizing Him as the Savior He was to be, the Son of God that He was. Bowing before another was no light thing for a Jewish person at that time. The Hebrews in Babylon had been put in the place of death for refusing to bow the knee to any other than God. This was a very guarded act for a Jew. That adds a certain enormity to the act of Mary.

It took steadfastness for Mary to maintain her devotional life in her heart. It took steadfastness for her to keep her eyes on Him and trust Him, no matter what. She did not turn from that devotion when those closest to her criticized her for sitting at His feet and soaking in His teachings. She did not turn when her beloved brother, the one who had introduced her to Christ, died. And on the evening of Mark 14, she did not let anything detour her from showing her devotion to this Christ, this Savior, this King of her life. It was not easy and it was not an action born out of carelessness or choosing a more secret way. Mary could have waited until all had left the place of feasting and asked Jesus and her brother to meet her in the secret place of the inner garden of their home. Surely Jesus would have come. He understood her heart. But she did the act in an open way, before the eyes of others, some of whom had not understood. She opened herself to criticism and misunderstanding. But her devotion directed each step of her journey into that place of feasting. Her devotion drove her to her knees.

I wonder how often we take the easy road in our own devotional lives. Do we purposefully choose to sit at Jesus' feet and soak in His Word? Do we spend quality time in prayer and praise? Or is it always easier to use the ten minutes of a devotional book, the quickly whispered prayers as we go out the door of a morning, the one service a month? Does that make us feel spiritual? Or should it leave us somehow lacking, with a hunger inside for more. We should not be satisfied with just the crumbs from the Master's table, but a full meal each day. The story of Mary and her life devotion to Christ should be a challenge to us. The total devotion of this woman is the memorial that speaks to our hearts! It was a memorial, also, that surely started to speak to others that were in the room that day. God may have urged Mary to walk into that room occupied by others as a testimony to them. Only some criticized and even of those that did, there was a lesson to be learned. It was the lesson of total devotion.

Others in Scripture have shown us deep lessons about devotion:

Read Nehemiah 1:1-2:8:
What did Nehemiah do when he saw a great need of his brethren in Jerusalem?

Was Nehemiah in great need himself at the time? (Hint: What was his position in life? Where did he live?)

How do you think the need of the other Jews became his own deep need?

Was the prayer and burden Nehemiah had in Nehemiah Chapter One short lived? (Hint - compare the time periods in the first verses of both Chapters One and Two.)

How does this speak of his devotion?

How did the devotion of Nehemiah affect his life?

How did the devotion of Nehemiah affect the life of the King and Queen of Babylon?

How did the devotion of Nehemiah affect the lives of the Jews at Jerusalem?

Think deeply: How does the devotion of Nehemiah affect your life?

Nehemiah's devotion helped set the stage for the return of Jerusalem's position as a city. The nation of Israel was being prepared as the place where one day Jesus would enter into that very city of Jerusalem, through those very walls rebuilt by Nehemiah's band. Nehemiah had a part in the preparations for our own redemption.

Think deeply again:
How could your devotional life affect those around you?

How could your devotional life affect future generations?

How could your devotional life affect our country?

Read Luke 2:21-35
How do we know that Simeon had a consistent, steadfast devotion to God?

What words are used in verse twenty-five to tell us about his devotion?

What message from God was Simeon able to receive because he was in a state of prayer on the morning of the day Mary and Joseph brought Jesus to the temple?

How much of a time margin do you think the old man Simeon had to meet Jesus that day?

How could neglecting prayer and devotion in our own lives hinder the messages God wants to give to our hearts?

Why is it we so often look back at an incident and realize how God would have had us act, instead of being prepared for the circumstance before it happened?

How was Simeon used in the lives of Mary and Joseph?

What did this meeting that day in the temple mean to Simeon?

How deeply did Simeon realize God's plan, as evidenced by verse 30-32?

How could daily consistent devotion help us in the matters of reassurance?

Read Luke 2:36-38

Anna was also a woman of deep, consistent devotion. How long had she been a widow?

What did she do with her widowhood?

What beautiful words "departed not" are in describing Anna. It was not only the temple that she did not depart from. Mention some other things that you think she did not depart from:

How could a widow or one who had suffered tragedy taken a different spiritual road that would have led her away from God?

What kind of things cause us, today, to depart from devotion to God?

Why should we not be surprised that Anna came "in that instant" that Simeon was praising God and holding the baby Jesus?

Do you think there is a connection between consistent devotional life and being "on time" for God's blessings?

What were the two things that Anna did when she saw Jesus, recorded in verse 38.

How are thanking and praising God part of a victorious devotional life?

How does this help us share Christ with others?

There is another thing that stands out in our study of Simeon and Anna. They were so given to devotion to God that they knew Jesus when they saw Him. They knew Him who to know is life eternal. They knew Him who gives redemption and salvation. They knew Him who gives blessing, peace and fulfillment to life. When we become fully devoted to Christ, one of the biggest blessings is that we will *KNOW* Him. Day by day, moment by moment, instant by instant, circumstance by circumstance, by trial and by blessing, we will know the presence of Christ with us as assuredly as if we were Simeon holding that sweet babe in his arms. To spend time with God in devotion is to experience the reality of His person in our lives.

It was this reality that impelled Mary of Bethany to walk through the door that evening, break the alabaster box and pour the liquid on Jesus, then humbly wipe it with her hair. I picture her as staying at His feet as He spoke to the others. With the words He spoke, Jesus declared that He knew the devotion of her life, her understanding of His Words and her courage in proclaiming Him as Lord. Her devotion was a cornerstone of the memorial that Christ built for her that day.

****

Cause me to hear thy lovingkindness in the morning;
for in thee do I trust:
cause me to know the way wherein I should walk;
for I lift up my soul unto thee.
Psalm 143:8

****

Softly, softly, as the day broke, Mary slid to her knees.
Quietly, reverently, she bowed her head and heart
     As she knelt still before His presence,
     As she did each morning, in the privacy of her room.

     She did not rush her thoughts, but quieted them instead.
     Slowly the burdens of the day came before her mind.
          She knelt there and gave them to the Lord.
          Peace filled her heart and she arose from her knees.

Calmly, joyfully, she stepped outside to meet the new day.
Praise filled her soul as she saw the sparkling of dew on the garden.
     Her heart lifted up, to the Lord of her life.
     Her thanksgiving and praise floated through the air.

Eyes alert, mind at ease, she listened at the breakfast table.
Gathering in all that brother Lazarus shared of God's Word.
     Still she sat drinking it all in,
     Remembering the words of Christ that day months ago.

Work done,
     Martha and Lazarus departed for Simon the Leper's house,
     Mary returned to her room,

to the coolness and stillness there.
Down she slid onto her knees, once again in deep prayer.
She knew what she had to do and when she should do it.
The peace in her heart told her so.
The gentle urging of the Spirit on her mind confirmed it.
The devotion in her soul secured it.
O Lord of my life,
Help me this night to show You
The love and devotion of my heart.
Take this gift of mine,
This Alabaster Box,
As a symbol of what I feel.
As an anointing beforehand of You.

Chapter Six
Give of Your Labor to God

Unto the angel of the church of Ephesus write;
These things saith he that holdeth the seven stars in his right hand,
who walketh in the midst of the seven golden candlesticks;
I know thy works…
Revelation 2:1-2a

At the very onset of the Revelation given to John the Apostle on the Isle of Patmos, we see Jesus. He is the One who walks in the midst of the seven golden candlesticks representing the seven churches of Revelation chapters Two through Three. The first proclamation that Christ makes to these churches, as recorded by John, is found in the simple phrase *I know thy works.* Down through the passage of time, the Lord knows all about us. Intricately woven into God's knowledge of our faith and motives, is the fact that He knows our works. This can be both sobering and encouraging. It is sobering to be fully aware that all we do, whether by faith or selfish service, is known by our God of what sort it is. But it is also encouraging, when others may not understand or even notice, that God knows what we have done.

Mary, that day, at the house of Simon the leper, in her quiet way would not have published what she was about to do. It was a labor of love for Christ. It was a work of faith and devotion. What she did by quiet determination, would be published by Christ as a testimony of her service to Him. She had done what she could, but she had also done it, when others had let such an opportunity pass them by. Indeed, Jesus does call it her *work:*

And being in Bethany in the house of Simon the leper, as he sat at meat,
there came a woman having an alabaster box of ointment of spikenard very precious;

and she brake the box and poured it on his head.
And there were some that had indignation…
And they murmured against her.
And Jesus said, Let her alone; why trouble ye her? She hath wrought
a good work on me.
Mark 14:3-6

In this chapter we will consider the importance of giving of our labor to the Lord. As the oil from the alabaster box was poured out, so our works need to be poured out day by day, even hour by hour, in consecration to the Lord who died on the Cross and stands between the seven golden candlesticks. The Lord, our Savior, Jesus Christ, is worthy of all our labor, whether easy or hard, common or extraordinary, of habitual duty or of spontaneous joy. Work is work. That is why the word is used. It is a labor. We have to put our hands to the plow to be used to break up the fallow ground, we have to open our mouths if we are to publish good tidings of peace, we have to organize our supplies if we are to provide for the needy. And we must get out the mop bucket and scrub brushes if we are to be good keepers at home. Truly life is not segmented. All is to be done as unto the Lord. That which some would consider menial and that which others would call spiritual are all to be done unto Him. The work of a mother at home is just as spiritual as the ministry of the missionary on a foreign field. It is a matter of heart devotion shown through our works. All must be done for the Lord.

In my imagination, I view Mary as one who treasured the things she learned deep in her heart. Not only had she learned the teachings of Jesus that day when she had sat at His feet as He taught, but she had doubtless learned other things. She had heard Martha's complaint that she had left the serving that day. I do not believe that would have fallen on a proud heart. It was not in Mary's gentle committed spirit to boast of sitting at Jesus' feet or to defend herself.

Now it came to pass, as they went, that he entered into a certain
village:

and a certain woman named Martha received him into her house.
And she had a sister called Mary, which also sat at Jesus feet, and
heard his word.
But Martha was cumbered about much serving,
and came to him, and said,
Lord, dost thou not care that my sister hath left me to serve alone?
bid her therefore that she help me.
Luke 10:38-40

Jesus clearly praised Mary for choosing *that good part, which shall not be taken away from her (Luke 10:42).* Her desire had been to learn more from Christ, but still there was the fact that Mary would have known she had upset her much loved sister. Martha seems to have been the oldest who provided for Mary's well being physically. Deep in her heart, Mary was assured of Jesus' love and commendation, yet also aware that she had left Martha with the *much serving.* Though Martha was reminded that her own choice had been to be *careful and troubled about many things (Luke 10:41),* she doubtless may have desired to be at Jesus' feet also, yet there had been a practical work to do. I wonder if that night, Mary did not lay on her bed considering the balance of life. "What if I had helped Martha more before the teaching started?" she may have thought. "Could I have been a better help meet to my sister and still have chosen the good part of being with Jesus as He taught?" The questions must have gone through her tender mind.

Perhaps the next morning, Mary arose early to greet her sister in the kitchen. Is it possible that she could have said, "Martha, is there anything I can do to help you today?" With a turn and a smile, I can envision Martha crossing the space between herself and Mary to hold her closely and say, "Thank you, Mary. Yes, there is much to do today. While we work together, would you share with me what you heard our Master teach yesterday?"

The balance of work and devotional dedication to the Lord

must always be uniquely intertwined in our lives. If one gets tangled or the weaving becomes uneven, then we may suffer loss. Our labor must be in direct strength as the faith of our devotion. The resulting fabric of our lives will be a beauty to behold and a testimony to the difference that Christ makes. Mary may have needed a "to do list." I always am more productive when I have one and adhere to it. It is not "The Dreaded List," but one of purpose and vision of what is possible. Some days, not all the labor is finished before bedtime. In my younger years, I would stay up until each item was crossed off the list. Now in my older years, I can seem to most often shift that item to the new list for the morning. God knows my heart. That is one of the reasons Jesus' comment concerning Mary's actions that day at Simon the leper's home so impressed me. *She hath done what she could. Mark 14:8a* These words bring comfort to my heart. Somedays I dream of doing more, but I am restricted by time, health or priorities. I can lay those things before my much loved Lord Jesus and know beyond the shadow of a doubt that He whispers to my heart, "You have done what you could today, dear daughter. Rest in Me, for I know thy works and the boundaries I have set for you."

Yet, once again, we are reminded that God does give us work to do! God reminds us that we are to be diligent in life.

Be thou diligent to know the state of thy flocks, And look well to thy herds. Proverbs 27:23

Seest thou a man diligent in his business? he shall stand before kings... Proverbs 22:29

And beside this, giving all diligence, add to your faith virtue; and to virtue knowledge..
II Peter 1:5

Yea, a man may say, thou hast faith, and I have works:

Shew me thy faith without works, and I will shew thee my faith by my works.
James 2:18

Even in the passage in James, there seems to be the idea of diligence in the believer's works that is desired. It is as if James is pleading, "Choose the better part of life's labor. Give of your works to the Master!"

Why do you think it is necessary to be diligent in your works?

What do you think is the application of James 2:18 to your own life?

How does diligence affect our testimony for Christ?

Why would it be important for our faith in Jesus Christ to be shown through our works? (and not just be the observance of a busy person who does good works outside of Christ's salvation):

"Trying to do the Lord's work in Your own strength
is the most confusing, exhausting, and tedious of all work.
But when you are filled with the Holy Spirit, then the ministry of
Jesus just flows out of you." Corrie Ten Boom

What do you think about this quote of Corrie Ten Boom?

Is there anything in your life that you feel you are doing in your own strength and not in the strength of the Holy Spirit?

Mary would have had a great Biblical illustration of the value of godly work done by a woman. It would have been found in the Old Testament teachings shared at her home, from the Book of Ruth. Faithful Ruth, who had proclaimed: *thy God [the God of Israel]my God. Ruth 1:16* In all that she decided in her heart and all that she did in her deeds, *she was stedfastly minded.. Ruth 1:18* That steadfastness did not end when the long journey to Bethlehem was completed, but continued day by day. When Ruth and her mother-in-law Naomi arrived, it was in the beginning of barley harvest. They must have lacked provisions, as it had been a long journey. Even if the home they occupied had been in the waiting, it would have been emptied perhaps of all provisions. Ruth did not beg or ask to be made a person of pity, instead she set to work to provide for her mother-in-law's needs as well as her own. She asked permission of Naomi to *go to the field, and glean ears of corn after him in whose sight I shall find grace. Ruth 2:2* Gleaning would not have been easy work. It was finding the left overs in part of the harvest fields that were set aside for that purpose. It was a God given commandment for the field's owner to leave parts of his harvested fields for those who were in need. It was a humbling position and a back-bending job to glean. Yet, day after day, Ruth followed at a safe distance from the reapers in that part of the field given for gleaning. She collected what was left over as sustenance for Naomi and herself. She labored, and her work and position were totally given over to the God who had become her God. She did so with all humility and grace, having asked: *I pray you, let me glean and gather after the reapers among the sheaves: so she came, and... continued even from the morning until* [the end of day]. *Ruth 2:7* She was selfless, diligent and obedient to God's law.

Mary would have learned that Ruth was rewarded for her labors, even if she had not sought to gain a reward. Boaz, the wealthy owner of the fields gave her this blessing: *The LORD recompense thy work, and a full reward be given thee of the LORD God of Israel, under whose wings thou art come to trust. Ruth 2:12* Her earthly rewards would also come to include a loving marriage and the honor of being the great grandmother of King David. God's mercy, grace and rewards are for all those who place their trust and their labors in Him.

Mary could have learned all that from her youth as she sat under the Biblical teaching of her brother Lazarus. Like Ruth, it seems that Mary's heart was to serve and to labor those things that were pleasing to God.

We today have not only the Scriptural examples of Ruth and of Mary, but the declarations of our Lord Jesus in Revelation chapters Two to Four, as He states what He knows of the works of the churches, and also what He would desire of them. The Lord knew their works and He knows our works! He knows if they are done in faith, in love, in commitment, in sacrifice. In references to the seven churches in Revelation, God declares that He knows if the labors of their hands match the faith of their hearts, if their patience in the work is wrought of the Holy Spirit, if the works are with the fervor of the first works of amazed dedication. He knew if they were faithful in their works to hold fast God's name and not to deny His faith. Of the works, He knew if they were done in love, by service to God, whether they were perfect, done when strength was almost gone, and whether they were cold or hot. That is quite a list of God's desire concerning the labors of His people.

Let us make a list of those motivational labors and apply them to our own lives. After all, we want to please the Lord with all our hearts and souls, with all our minds and labors. As all Scripture is given by inspiration and for our learning, let us glean from these declarations in the Book of Revelation in order to gain sustenance for our own labors of love for our God.

Done in faith:

The Apostle Paul gave thanks to God for those in the Thessalonian church: *Remembering without ceasing your work of faith...1 Thessalonians 1:13.* Their work of faith was not only noteworthy, but one of the proofs that the Gospel *came not unto you in word only, but in power.* Again, in II Thessalonians 1:11, Paul prays: *Wherefore also we pray always for you, that our God would count you worthy of this calling, and fulfill all the good pleasure of his goodness, and the work of faith with power.* The faith that saved these members of the church in Thessalonica also motivated and empowered their labors for the Lord. They had become examples to others in Macedonia and Achaia. As in the Book of James, their faith was evidenced by their works. They trusted God to enable them to do that which they could not have done before, to please Him. II Thessalonians 1:12 declares that because of these works... *the name of our Lord Jesus Christ may be glorified in you, and ye in him...* What an amazing wonder salvation is! Flowing from the saving grace of God should be works done in faith that bring Him pleasure and glorify Him before others. Oh, that we would join hand with heart alongside those that have gone before us, in bringing glory to our Lord and trusting Him with our works.

Lord,
I need Your power and work of faith in my life to enable me to serve You.

Done in love:

In I Thessalonians 1:3, Paul mentions his prayers of praise for the believers' *labour of love... in the sight of God and our Father.* Those things that they did were seen of God. The Lord honored their love shown through their works. In our families, especially, we often do love deeds. How much more should we honor our God, who is our Father, with those special works that say from our heart, "I love You, Lord." When we hear of a ministry in the church that involves labor, it is that love of the Lord that should impel us onward to do that task which may be new to us, but of need in the church. Hebrews 6:10 states: *For God is not unrighteous to forget your work and labour of love, which ye have shewed toward his name, in that ye have ministered to the saints, and do minister.* As with Ruth and with Mary, so God is with each of us to remember our labor done in love! The love we have for God should overflow to reach others in love by our deeds.

Lord,
Help me to grow in love for You every day. Help that love to naturally show forth in the work I do for You and for others.
Help the others to see You in this ministry of love.

Done with commitment:

Commitment requires a certain totality of holding fast to that which we have placed in God's hands. There are many verses that urge us to *Hold fast the form of sound words... II Timothy 1:12* We are not to let go of the words of salvation and godly living. That power of God is what *saved us, and called us with an holy calling, not according to our* [own] *works, but according to his own purpose and grace... II Timothy 1:9* God's purposed works of grace working in and through us, what a marvelous truth! If our all is committed to God, we can perform those works! Out of commitment will come blessed labor for the Lord. Isaiah 1:19 declares God's blessing on committed works: *If ye be willing and obedient, ye shall eat the good of the land:*

Lord,
Steady my heart and let me be increasingly committed to You. Help each labor that I do be a reflection of that earnest steadfastness that comes with commitment to the task You place within my sphere of work.

Done with a sacrificial motivation:

One of the primary commands to Israel involves spiritual motivations for sacrifices of labor: *And now, Israel, what doth the LORD thy God require of thee, but to fear the LORD thy God, to walk in all his ways, and to love him, and to serve the LORD thy God with all thy heart and with all thy soul. Deuteronomy 10:12.* It has been said that the work that costs us nothing is not a work of honor. Sometimes we must choose to sacrifice of our time, money and choices in order to honor the Lord with our work. The God who sees our motivations surely will reward those labors.

Lord,
Sometimes life seems to be so easy
and the moments just fly by.
But it is often in those difficult times of choice,
when You see the sacrifices that are made,
that we can find the most joy.

Laboring without fainting:

And let us not be weary in well doing: for in due season we shall reap, if we faint not. Galatians 6:9 How many deeds for the Lord have been left unfinished because the workers became weary in the doing? How many have turned back when the ground became rocky and the plow hard to guide? Even in our everyday lives, often we cast aside that work which seems too hard to do. The Christian who labors on, even into the twilight, will find new strength when their almost fainting hearts are renewed by faith.

Lord,
So often I can feel my own strength start to wane. It is then
that I so need Your strength and Your hand clasped around
mine, so that the labor will be completed in Your time.
On the Cross You cried, "It is finished."
You stayed the course for my soul's sin payment.

Help me to stay the course in my service to You,
for love's payment.

Done with godly patience:

To the church of Ephesus in Revelation 2:2-3, the Lord mentions two times that He knew their labors and their patience. There was much need for patience in their ministries for Christ. False philosophies, persecution and evil tried to invade the young church. But the spirit of patience was their stronghold of faith. With patient labor, the church, despite many failures, held on to their faith. When all around us seems to be caving in and temptations mount, it is this same spirit of patience which can guide us steadfastly to trust in God's outcome, to hold fast to true faith and to labor on. *But that on the good ground are they, which in an honest and good heart, having heard the word, keep it, and bring forth fruit with patience. Luke 8:15. But in all things approving ourselves as the ministers of God, in much patience, in afflictions, in necessities, in distresses, II Corinthians 6:4. For ye have need of patience, that, after ye have done the will of God, ye might receive the promise. Heb 10:36.*

Lord,
One of our greatest needs is to access the fruit of patience
from the Holy Spirit.
You gave us all we need at salvation in the area of patience,
but how often we forget.
When we forget, we try to hurry to do the work in our own
strength. Getting frustrated, we can even give way to anger.
Help us, help me, to realize the great gift You have given us
in the Fruit of Patience
which gives peace and joy in our work.

Done like as to the first works for God:

"The first works for God." I wonder how many of us should think back to what were the first works that we did for God after our salvation. Perhaps we were so young in the Lord, like newborn babes in Christ, we did not realize that what we were doing were "works for God!" The responses of our hearts seemed to naturally flow to the performance of that which was a labor for the Lord. We suddenly saw it as part of our new life, an outgrowth of that which had changed within. I can remember that my "first work for God" after receiving the Lord as my Savior on a college campus one evening, was to read His Word. As had been suggested to me, I began at the Book of John, but not being told where to stop, I just kept reading and marveling. My room mates came in from their dates and I knew I just had to share what had happened to me! I did the work of an evangelist without even realizing it. It was because of joy. There is that marvel, joy and spontaneity that comes with the first works we did for God that we must never lose. Nothing about the Christian life should ever become common place! That is what God wanted the Christians He was instructing in Revelation to realize. He did not want them to lose that which was precious and fruitful! In Matthew 6:33, Jesus declares: *But seek ye first the kingdom of God, and his righteousness...* First in priority, first in our hearts. Acts 26:20 recounts Paul's witness to King Agrippa concerning what were his first works unto God after "the heavenly vision." He went out and declared the Gospel that could save souls: *But shewed first unto them of Damascus, and at Jerusalem, and throughout all the coasts of Judaea, and then to the Gentiles, that they should repent and turn to God, and do works meet for repentance.* Paul knew intimately the fervor of the first works done for God. There are three words in Acts 26:20 that help us to understand that fervency. *First* meaning in time and place but also in rank of highest honor. *Do* means to act and to accomplish, to be busy about the doing. *Meet* means to be worthy, having the value in our performance and doing that which is befitting of our station. God would desire that we would <u>first</u> <u>do</u> the things that are <u>meet</u> for servants of the Most High God.

Lord,
Help each of us to remember that gratefulness for the new
birth of salvation and how it overflowed
to our first works done for God.
Help us never to be complacent
or think that we have fully completed our course
while we still have breath to serve.
Renew to us the fervency and naturalness of first works.

<u>Done to hold fast God's name and not deny His faith:</u>

Revelation 3:3 is given as a command: *Hold fast...* We are not to let our labors weaken. We are to hold fast! We are not to cast them to the side or let them slip from our hands. We are to hold fast! In I Thessalonians 5:21, we are commanded to *prove all things; hold fast that which is good.* To not perform labor for God is to cast off that which is good. Our hands would be left empty and there would be a void in our lives. Hebrews 3:6, 4:14 and 10:23 tell us to hold fast our confidence, rejoicing in hope and our profession of faith without wavering. As I was writing this, I stopped to clench my hands tightly in a holding mode. It was amazing how much I could feel that conscious clasping of each hand. I could feel the power such "labor" produced. Hold fast!

Lord,
Help me to have the strength needed to hold fast in the work
You have given me to do.
Thank You, that You are the Judge of my holding power
and the Supplier.
Let me never think that I am not able to hold fast.
Let me realize that You are encircling my hands
in the doing of Thy work.

Done with a servant's heart:

It is an honor to be called a servant of Christ. There is no groveling or hanging of our heads in that position. It is gifted to us at salvation. To be in the service of the Almighty God, the Creator of Heaven and Earth, is a privilege. Every day, we should seek to serve Him who loved us so much that He died for us. Think of the pure joy there is in that service. To work for Him who climbed Calvary's Hill for us. The immensity of that thought should humble our hearts. Ephesians 6:7 speaks of that work for Christ: *with good will doing service as to the Lord; and not to men.* Men may ignore servants, but Christ is ever aware of each one of us. Men may demean servants, but Christ gives us the privilege of being called the children of God. Therefore, we can understand the plea of Hebrews 12:28: *...let us have grace, whereby we may serve God acceptably with reverence and godly fear.* To expand the wording, the writer of Hebrews is encouraging us to have servants' hearts in our labors for God with joy, pleasure and delight, ministering with deeds of homage and worship to our Lord, in a manner pleasing to Him in respect and reverence. Those definitions of the words of Hebrews 12:28 should challenge our servants' hearts to increase our labors.

Lord,
I often think of that Heavenly mansion
You are preparing for me.
And then I think of the marvel of this place
and time of dwelling
that You have granted to me to serve
as Your servant on this earth.
Help me to do so with a loyal servant's heart.
Help my labor be done at Your command.

Done as unto perfection:

The word perfection usually means to do those things that are of maturity. As we grow in the Lord, our deeds should grow in perfection. To those that are mature, God calls: *Not slothful in business; fervent in spirit; serving the Lord. Romans 12:11.* There is a song line: "The longer I serve Him, the sweeter it grows." To serve Christ, striving for a maturity in that service, and also in the beauty of a task well done, is a perfection seen by others and by God. There is an importance in making certain our tasks are done well.

Lord,
Work in Your house is always
to be done in the highest manner of perfection possible.
What others view of our earthly places of worship
should reflect the honor we give to You.
What others view as the earthly tabernacle of our lives,
should show forth the glory of Your name!
Help me to serve as unto perfection.
Let my labors show forth the perfection of all that You are!

Done even when our own strength is almost gone:

There have been those times when we can feel our own earthly strength start to give way as we labor in the harvest field. It is just at that moment when we often feel the strength of the Holy Spirit lift our weary hands to finish the task. God enjoins us to redeem the times! *So teach us to number our days, that we may apply our heart unto wisdom. Psalm 90:12. Redeeming the time, because the days are evil. Wherefore be ye not unwise, but understanding what the will of the Lord is. Ephesians 5:16-17. Walk in wisdom toward them that are without, redeeming the time. Colossians 4:5.* There is a wisdom and purpose in redeeming the time and in continuing on when our strength is almost gone.

Lord,
Let me not fail in finishing the course You have set before me.
Done with the temperature of fervor:

...let him labour, working with his hand the thing which is good... Ephesians 4:28. Whatsoever thy hand findeth to do, do it with thy might... Ecclesiastes 9:10a. Works that are just lukewarm are not the kind that we should be performing for our God. He is ever faithful and true. He is ever upholding us with His love. He never did a work halfway. When Jesus died on the Cross, He said, "It is finished." Each day of Creation, God could say that it was good!

Lord,
Let us labor with a fervor of intensity that concentrates
all our abilities to Your service.
Let us know in our hearts that we have let You work
through us what is good.
Let us finish that which we have been given
by Thy divine grace to do.

The first woman, Eve, was given the godly honor of being a help meet to Adam and they were to keep the Garden. It was a labor to do. Even after the Fall and the expulsion from that beautiful place of peace, God also gave her labors to do. They would not be as easy perhaps, nor always filled with triumph, but they were labors that she was to do as unto the Lord. It is not often that we think of the great joy and honor there is in our labors, but we ought to be aware that every day, in every way, we can labor for the Lord. Though we are not in the Garden of Eden, but in the modern world, we can still do labors that are motivated by love for our Lord. Work can be blessed and a blessing.

Mary, I would imagine, had work that she needed to do in her everyday life. Perhaps she was to be serving or washing dishes or cooking or maintaining the order of the servants in the home. There are many possibilities, but each was her labor of the moment. Each could be done begrudgingly or with joy and honor to the Lord. Serving could be done as a ministry to others, letting them see the peace and purpose of her life. Maintaining the servants in a home, could demonstrate to them love and appreciation. Even washing dishes could be done with a focus on perfection and standards of dignity. In our lives each day, we each have labors of the moment. We need to watch for them and claim them as the treasures of service for Christ that they can be. That which might have been drudgery to us yesterday, can become joy and victory today when that labor is given to the Lord.

Often, we "equate" labors for the Lord to those of the Pastor preaching, the missionary serving on the foreign field, the soloist on Sunday morning. But truly each labor, each work, each deed laid before us is equally needful of spiritual emphasis. Within a dedicated home, the lesson of labors done for Christ and joy in His service can affect generations to come. Many a little head bowed in prayer for salvation has experienced grace within the confines of the family home. Let us strive to labor in that home to bring glory to our Lord. Let our labors bring a peace and comfort of commitment to service. Let each of us labor for Christ.

Mary in the quiet of the enclosed room of dining did what may have been the most memorable service of labor for her in her life. Christ assured her and the others that what she had done would be spoken of for generations. Mary's work that day was the pouring of the precious ointment on Jesus. It was a work well done.

****

Thoughtful Meditation and Questions

We each have different "jobs" to do in life:
1)   Make a list of some of the jobs that you feel are uniquely part of your life.

2)   Which of these jobs do you consider to be your main "work" in life?

3)   Looking at the list, which labors do you find joy in?

4)   How can you use each of these "jobs" to honor Christ in a more vibrant way?

5)   Are there any tasks that are taking too much time away from that which you need to accomplish to make your life more Christ centered?

6)   How could you change the time expenditure or focus to allow more spiritual labors?

7)   Is there any "labor" in your life that you have found you have been performing in your own strength that you would desire to be done as unto the Lord?

8)   How do you think this would change your life? Your witness? Your joy?

****
Morning dawn formed a shaft of light that fell
Softly on Mary's hands,
Warming them
After the cool of the Spring night.
Her eyes opened in the awareness of the early morning

And the first sight
Were her hands,
Wrapped in that early light of day.

Her mind rested there in thought.
Lord, what would You desire
Of my hands today?
I know there is work to do.
Let me do it for You.
Strengthen them for the tasks ahead.
Help me to please You
And my family
And those around me.

When it comes time to do that which You have laid on my heart,
Keep my hands steady,
Help them to hold the alabaster box securely,
Let me not fumble in opening the clasp
And pouring out the ointment,
As I would pour out my love
On Him who deserves all
My devotion,
Labor and service.

I do not understand it completely,
But I know,
He will pour out
The payment for my sins
With His life.
Help these hands to ointment Him
For His burial,
Err I might lose the chance given
This day.

Thank You,
For anointing my hands,
With the rays of Your light,
and waking me so gently to this day of service
Given me to perform for You.

****

...a woman that feareth the LORD, she shall be praised.
Give her of the fruit of her hands;
And let her own works praise her in the gates.
Proverbs 31:30b-31

Therefore, my beloved brethren,
Be ye stedfast, unmoveable, always abounding in the work of the
Lord,
Forasmuch as ye know that your labour is not in vain in the Lord.
I Corinthians 15:58

Chapter Seven
Give of Your Reward and Honor to the Master

Give unto the LORD the glory due unto his name;
Worship the LORD in the beauty of holiness.
Psalm 29:2

In six chapters we have thought of Mary of Bethany and her act of devotion to her Lord that day of the feast at the house of Simon the leper. We have pictured her breaking the alabaster box of beauty filled with precious ointment to anoint her Master, Jesus. She did this in preparation for His soon burial. She had listened and understood that He had come to die for her. She had surely done what the words of Psalm 29:2 sang in the heart of her worship. She had come to give unto the Lord Jesus the glory due to His name! She had come to worship Him in the beauty of holiness from her deepest heart of faith. All we have stated about Mary would show that she did not do this for self-reward or self-honor. All the honor of her act was to Christ that day.

What a beautiful act of worship and honor Mary had done. Let us read again the account of that time, thinking of Mary's devotion to the Lord:

Mark 14:3-9
And being in Bethany in the house of Simon the leper, as he sat at meat,
there came a woman having an alabaster box of ointment of spikenard very precious;
and she brake the box, and poured it on his head.
And there were some that had indignation within themselves, and said,
Why was this waste of the ointment made?

For it might have been sold for more than three hundred pence, and
have been given to the poor.
And they murmured against her.
And Jesus said, Let her alone; why trouble ye her?
She hath wrought a good work on me.
For ye have the poor with you always,
and whensoever ye will ye may do them good:
but me ye have not always.
She hath done what she could:
she is come aforehand to anoint my body to the burying.
Verily I say unto you,
Wheresoever this gospel shall be preached
throughout the whole world,
this also that she hath done shall be spoken of for a memorial of her.

The emotions of that evening should be very real in our hearts. Some did not understand what had just happened before their eyes, and they criticized. But God would allow us the privilege of understanding today. We can hear the echo of Jesus' praise of her deed. We can treasure the recognition of her good work. We can realize that Jesus set up a spiritual memorial of Mary's acts that day. Memorials were very important in the life of Israel. Those listening to Jesus' honor given to Mary would have been struck with the greatness of that which He gave to her. He said, *this also that she hath done shall be spoken of for a memorial of her.* In using the word "memorial", Jesus would have called to the Jewish mind the great memorials of their faith already instituted by God.

Let us look up some pivotal memorials of the Jewish faith and comment on them:
Exodus 12:13-14:

Exodus 16:31-34:

Exodus 28:1-3, 9-12:

Numbers 15:37-41:

Number 16:35-40:

Joshua 4:1-7:

Joshua 24:14-27:

Think of the seriousness of these memorials set up for Israel. Now think of what is the one memorial set up for us as Christians: The Lord's Supper.

And he took bread, and gave thanks, and brake it, and gave it unto them, saying, This is my body which is given for you: this do in remembrance of me.
Luke 22:19

...this do ye, as oft as ye drink it, in remembrance of me.
For as often as ye eat this bread, and drink this cup, ye do shew the Lord's death till he come.
I Corinthians 11:24b-25

How did the realization of the seriousness of the memorials set for Israel help in your understanding of the memorial of the Lord's Supper?

Why do you think Christ instituted this memorial?

Mention how you personally feel when you participate in the Lord's Supper:

What impact should the Lord's Supper have upon the children who watch or partake?

What lessons and memorial do you desire for these little ones to learn?

The remembrance of what Jesus did when He died on the Cross for our sins is our spiritual memorial of faith. To become a Christian, we must believe that He is Lord and that He died and rose again: *That if thou shalt confess with thy mouth the Lord Jesus, and shalt believe in thine heart that God hath raised him from the dead, thou shalt be saved. Romans 10:9.* God gives us a reminder of that which we have believed and that which Jesus has done, the remembrance of The Lord's Supper, the taking of the bread and wine to symbolize the body and blood of our Lord, given for us on Calvary. What a blessed memorial! We do not have to travel to the Jordan River to see the stones set up for a remembrance of God's miracle in the crossing of Israel in the time of Joshua. Wherever we are in our life journey, God's remembrance of Christ's death is there, set as sure as the Rock of that firm foundation which is Jesus! The seriousness of our remembrance should be intently real each time we partake with our brethren.

How much the memorial of Mary of Bethany was honored by Jesus that day should amaze us. In the quiet personal act of devotion and honor, an anointing of the One who would die for her sins, was a memorial to stand in the Biblical record. There were no stones set by the riverside, or pillars by a temple. The statement in Scripture of the Lord's honor is that memorial in God's remembrance of her act. What greater honor could there ever be for Mary?

There are Scriptural mentions of memorials for the faithful. Comment on the ones listed below:

Blessed is the man that feareth the LORD, that delighteth greatly in his commandments... Surely he shall not be moved for ever: the righteous shall be in everlasting remembrance... his heart is fixed, trusting in the LORD. His heart is established... Psalm 112:1-8

Sing... for the LORD hath comforted his people... [the Lord saith] yet, will I not forget thee. Behold, I have graven thee upon the palms of my hands... Isaiah 49:13-16

In all these things and more, God grants memorials to the faithful servants who trust in Him. We, also, can be counted among those who are so blessed. There is a constant of faithfulness that must be met and a love for God in our hearts that honors Him above all others. He must be the One that is set as a memorial within our spiritual hearts.

How easily it can be for some to turn away from faithfulness to seek self-honor and self-rewards. I do not think that at any moment of the evening of our study that Mary desired an earthly reward for what she was to do or dreamed that any would be given.

She did not seek to have acclaim or a reimbursement for the alabaster box and the ointment poured out. She did not announce her arrival with trumpets or cymbals. She just quietly came in the room to do the private act of honor and reward to Christ. That is what the criticizers did not understand. She did not seek to sell her possession; she came only to give it totally. Mary did not even have to beg the reward of Jesus' understanding and acknowledgment of her gift. It was enough to know in her heart that there would surely be the silent reward of His understanding and acceptance of the gift. Jesus did not stay her hand, nor move away. He patiently let her continue her worship of honor for His coming sacrifice. That would have been enough for Mary, I am certain. Yet Jesus abundantly gave her the reward recorded in Mark 14:9: *Verily I say unto you, Wheresoever this gospel shall be preached throughout the whole world, this also that she hath done shall be spoken of for a memorial of her.* Through all ages this declaration in honor of what she had done will be spoken of and remembered. We can almost imagine that even in heaven a lovely locket will hang around her neck with the engraving: "This is she that hath done what she could. This is she that poured the ointment on My head. Blessing and Honor on her soul!"

The Scripture tells in a parable about the words the faithful will hear when they have finished their work: *Well done, thou good and faithful servant... enter thou into the joy of thy lord. Matthew 25:21, 23* In the parable, Jesus is teaching the lesson of faithful servants entrusted by their master with duties to perform. Their reward is found in these gracious words of the master when he returns to inspect their faithfulness. The parable is also a picture of our Heavenly Lord entrusting us with duties to perform on earth. He who knows and sees all, is a bounteous Rewarder of those that serve Him. Sometimes the rewards are earthly and sometimes they come in Glory. In the parable, the immediate reward was the commendation of the lord to his faithful servants.

Let us place ourselves into the position of the servants and God as our Master. Is God's reward of those words *Well done* enough for us or do we still look at what others might say and do to honor us in this life. Even if we are never praised on this earth by others, we can be faithful. Our later public acclaim will be in Heaven given by God's own voice! Think on that and the marvel of its truth. God Himself, as our Master, will acknowledge that which we have done to give honor and reward to His name by our obedience on earth. We must each come to the point of saying, "It is enough to hear those words from my Lord someday: *Well Done*! And to see the smile in His eyes and the love in His look." Even here on earth, it should be enough to feel the witness of the Holy Spirit within, giving us the assurance that *It Is Well With My Soul.*

It was not the coinage that was gained by the servants in the parable of Matthew 25, but the faithfulness to their master and the entrusted duty to his "kingdom," that brought the reward. Matthew 25:14, states clearly that this parable was like unto the kingdom of Heaven. Even if we are given talents, is the reward in seeing them shine for others to see and for us to possess gain from, or is it in the honor we can give to our Heavenly Master by the use of those talents? In many a small church, there are vocalists of great talent who are moved to honor their Lord in the use of their voices. In the world, there are those who use their voices only to advance their own careers and gain earthly fame, even if they have to turn their backs on godly standards and bring dishonor to God. Which is of greatest value in eternity?

Read John 5:44.
Comment on the importance of the word "not" in that verse.

Could we receive acclaim from others and still give God the glory?

Can you think of any examples of this in real life today?

There is a book written many years ago that deals with the importance of seeking God's kingdom's glory in our life on earth. For many years, that book was the best-selling Christian book after the Bible. It is called *In His Steps* by Charles Sheldon and was first published in 1896. The full title of the book is *In His Steps: What Would Jesus Do?* In this intriguing fictional book, Charles Sheldon presents the reader with the lives of people in a large church who are suddenly confronted with the question of whether they are truly living their lives to honor Christ or themselves. Those that find true peace and grow in their faith are those that commit their talents, works, strivings for success and life goals to God. Their prayer becomes, "What would Jesus do in this situation?" Jesus truly gave the answer in John 6:38: *For I came down from heaven, not to do mine own will, but the will of him that sent me.*

How does the personal application of the principles of John 6:38 affect your life decisions today?

Can you think of some area of your life where you need to be more aware of how Jesus would react and serve?

How does the world try to call to us to walk in the steps of a worldly path toward success and fame?

Do you think there is often emptiness in such striving?

Can you describe the fullness of peace that God can give for those choosing His way over that of the world?

In Charles Sheldon's book, there were those that did not choose the path of honoring their Lord. They were either too engrained with worldly strivings, thought future Heavenly reward was not to be compared with present earthly acclaim, or were weak in their faith. There were even those who realized they were not truly saved and part of the Body of Christ. They had chosen to refuse God's offer of salvation and, instead, had chosen temporary "worldly success." Some failed even in life's goals. In the book, there were the few who continued to have worldly success, but who in God's eyes truly failed in the choices that were most important, those that were of honor.

Read the parable of Luke 12:15-21

Think of what others may have thought about the wealth of the rich man that kept increasing?

How do you know this man did not honor God in the achieving of his wealth (Hint: verse 19)?

Where are we to lay up our treasures?

Could the rich man have rejoiced in the bounty of the harvest and still honored God?

Read Luke 12:22-31, as Jesus continues the theme of the parable.

Have you memorized Luke 12:31? Write it out and put in a prominent place in your home to remind you of the importance of honoring God and not self. Let us be "God Seekers," not self-seeking in our lives!

To seek to honor God in every deed, action, word and thought is the true cure to striving only for self-honor and acclaim. Read the words of this ancient hymn and reflect on the honor and praise that we should give to Christ:

All Glory, Laud and Honor

Repeated Refrain:
All glory, laud, and honor, to thee, Redeemer, King,
To whom the lips of children made sweet hosannas ring.

Verse 1: Thou art the King of Israel, thou David's royal Son,
Who in the Lord's name comest, the King and Blessed One.
(Refrain)

Verse 2: The company of angels are praising thee on high,
And we with all creation in chorus make reply.
(Refrain)

Verse 3: The people of the Hebrews with psalms before thee went;
Our prayer and praise and anthems before thee we present.
(Refrain)

Verse 4: To thee, before thy passion, they sang their hymns of praise;
To thee, now high exalted, our melody we raise.
(Refrain)

Verse 5: Thou didst accept their praises; accept the prayers we bring,
Who in all good delightest, thou good and gracious King.
(Refrain)

Write a reflection on the honor and praise we should give to Christ:

There is a very convicting verse containing Jesus' estimation of those that seek self-honor and not honor from God. He was speaking to the Jews that sought to kill Him, as early as John Chapter Five. In the midst of His declaration to them, Jesus said:

But I know you, that ye have not the love of God in you.
I am come in my Father's name, and ye receive me not;
If another shall come in his own name, him ye will receive.
How can ye believe, which receive honor one of another,
And seek not the honour that cometh from God only?
John 5:42-44

The word "not" is used three times in this quoted passage. Find each one and comment on its context in relationship to the unbelieving Jews, and then apply to our lives today:

1)

2)

3)

There is a transitory element in earthly honor. Often times, there are individuals that receive acclaim and praise from men, but the second that they make a mistake or fail to raise up their fan base, that honor ceases. There are those who have won medals and awards, later to have them taken away for a discovered infraction. They were cheered in victory and criticized in loss. Some military leaders have, in the past, claimed the devotion and idolization of the masses, but when they were brought to defeat, there was the desertion of people's loyalties. Even the entertainment idols of yesteryear are soon forgotten for the new trends and performers. It seems that the honor and praise of others can fly quickly by like an elusive dragonfly. What looks beautiful is soon lost in the swirl of public opinion.

But the pure love of God never fails! The honor of God for the faithful will stand like the pillars of the Heavenly temple. *Him that overcometh will I make a pillar in the temple of my God... Revelation 3:12.* There is a solidarity and permanence in the honor God gives.

Strengthen your heart and mind, dear Christian, and seek the things of God.

****

He that followeth after righteousness, and mercy findeth life,
righteousness, and honour.
Proverbs 21:21

By humility and fear of the LORD are riches, and honour, and life.
Proverbs 22:4

If ye then be risen with Christ, seek those things which are above,
where Christ sitteth on the right hand of God.
Set your affections on things above, not on things on the earth.
Colossians 3:1-2
****

The feast was done, the visitors had departed.
Lazarus joined his sisters at the gate to the street.
There was a soft hush in the air,
The moonlight lit the path ahead.
Lazarus felt it was a time of blessing from the Lord.
The end of a special day.

He turned his eyes Heavenward and marveled,
The God who had made the sparkling stars above,

Had uniquely fashioned Mary,
Whose quiet deed shone in his mind,
Stored in his memory like the precious alabaster
Had glowed as Mary lifted it up.

What an act of praise that had been at the feast;
The quiet unexpected raising of her delicate hands
Wrapped securely around the box
Broken to pour out its contents
On the head of the Lord of all Glory and Creation.
Mary had anointed Jesus for His burial.

He remembered the Master's words spoken clearly,
Putting to silence the criticizers, as the oil continued
Its journey down to Jesus' feet,
On its pathway of honor.
Gentle Mary had never left her post of worship
As the Lord Himself gave her praise.

Thank You, Lord, for these two sisters You have given,
Each for Your praise and honor in my life,
One knowing Your majesty in Resurrection,
The other praising Your sacrifice in Death.
What more can I do, Lord, to show my knowledge
Of You, the One who raised me?

I will set You for a memorial in my heart,
I will praise Your honor before others,
I will give of what You place in my hands
As a gift of love for Your mighty grace.

Help me, Master, to not seek my own honor,
As others still comment as I pass their way.

"He is the one Jesus raised to life,
He is surely to be honored," they say.
But it is You, Jesus, You alone, that is to be praised.
Help me to testify of You!
Let all honor and praise be to You
Who formed the heavens
And the stars above.
Help me to tell of Your mighty love.

Chapter Eight
Give of your talents and abilities to God

All for Jesus! All for Jesus! All my being's ransomed powers:
All my thoughts and words and doings, All my days and all my hours.
Let my hands perform His bidding. Let my feet run in His ways:
Let my eyes see Jesus only. Let my lips speak forth His praise.
Since my eyes were fixed on Jesus, I've lost sight of all beside;
So enchained my spirit's vision, Looking at the Crucified.
O what wonder! How amazing! Jesus, glorious King of kings,
Deigns to call me His beloved, lets me rest beneath His wings.
All for Jesus   **Mary D. James**

Even every one that is called by my name: for I have created him for
my glory,
I have formed him; yea, I have made him.
Isaiah 43:7

We do not know much about Mary's personal talents or abilities. We know that she was a good listener. She is recorded as sitting at the feet of Jesus and listening as He taught. We know that she understood that Jesus was to die and be buried, as she poured out the ointment from the Alabaster box in advance to anoint Him for His burial. We know that when others gathered around the tomb of her brother Lazarus, mourning and lamenting, she was to be found inside the house. We can make assumptions about her personality, but we do not know all about her. We do not know if she could sing or sew. We do not know if she wove baskets or painted tiles. We do not know if she baked fine cakes or had a bountiful garden. But this we do know, God formed her for His glory.

It is just the same with you and me today. Each one of us was formed for God's glory! That is an overwhelming thought! It is a challenge that should speak to our hearts each day. Inside our minds, we should say, "This is the day that the Lord has made, how can I give Him glory today?" Then as we live each moment, the challenge should echo back: "Give Him glory today!" Mary James wrote the words to one of my favorite hymns "All for Jesus." Our all does not just include our possessions, our time, our destiny, our labor, our devotion, but so much more. One of the areas of our "all" is found in giving God that which He has created in each of us, our personalities and our talents. Tied uniquely to these things that make each of us unique, is that which God imparts to us at salvation, our spiritual gifts. God truly created each of us for His glory. He formed us and made us to serve Him. But we can only do this in the fulness He desires for our lives when we give to Him of our talents and gifts to be used for His Glory.

God placed us uniquely in each life situation. Where we live, where we walk down the street, where we converse with others, are all life opportunities that can and should be used for Him. Oh, what Glory that will be when we meet Him face to face in Heaven and then fully understand all that He formed for our lives. Oh, what Glory it can be when we experience that unique weaving of our lives here on earth to be used for Heavenly purposes. God does have a wonderful plan for our lives. We may not always recognize or utilize it, but we can be assured that His desire is for us to walk in the paths He has designed for us. Just as a vehicle is equipped to travel the highways in safety and in fullest potential, so God designed "instruments" and "equipment" to guide our navigation systems to travel His pathway set before us in victory and in our fullest God-given potential. May this chapter help us to think on those things that would bring Him glory in our walk.

What spiritual gift or gifts do you think you have been given?

What do you think are some of your strongest character traits?

What do you think are some of your weakest character traits?

In the late 1800's, Dwight L. Moody held many an evangelistic revival meeting in England and Scotland. There is the story told of a town to which Mr. Moody was to visit that had been rife with sinful practices and cold hearts toward God. In that town lived an elderly Christian woman, confined to her bed due to severe disabilities. It was laid on her heart to pray for Mr. Moody and the meetings, especially those in her home town. Unable to do much else, the dear lady labored in prayer from her bed. When the first meeting was held, observers had doubted of any spiritual decisions to be made, despite the fact that it was the renowned evangelist Moody speaking. But during the message, many people started to weep and, at the end, there were a great many decisions made. In fact, the times of the meetings were extended in that town and more came to salvation and rededication. Moody had marveled at God's blessings on the meetings. One of the local pastors related to Moody that there was this bed ridden lady at the edge of town that had labored in prayer for him at every meeting time. Moody went to visit her and pray with her. That night at the public meeting, he is said to have declared that the prayer ministry of that dear lady did more for souls in her town than all his preaching. In fact, Moody tearfully realized that the victories won, were won because of the power of prayer by that lady. She had done what she could. And she did it with the gift of prayer imparted to her by God's precious Spirit. Others may have thought she had no talents or gifts that could be given to God, but her sensitive heart knew that her duty, privilege and gift was simply to pray. That sacrifice of herself totally to God was a mighty weapon used for God's glory. The impact it had on Dwight L. Moody was to reap many rewards in future services as he was more keenly aware of God's power of prayer. Her gift was perhaps greater than all the talented singers in the British Isles of that day, for it was a gift totally given by and then given back to God.

Look up the following verses relating to gifts from God to individuals and comment on each one:
Romans 12:5-8:

I Corinthians 4:6-7:

I Corinthians 12:1, 4-12:

Ephesians 4:1-7, 11-12:

What common truths did you find in the above verses?

Read Ephesians 4:15-16. Comment on how they affect your understanding of spiritual gifts:

There is a sacred interaction of the spiritual gifts given to each individual with the whole of the local body of believers. The gifts are to be ministered realizing that they each came from the grace of God. The same God that redeemed us by grace gives spiritual gifts. They are all of Him and for His glory! None is a product of ourselves, just as salvation is not something that we earn or work for, it is the gift of God, the greatest gift in our lives. How great then should we view spiritual gifts!

These gifts are given to be used to edify the body and to speak of the grace and glory of our Lord. How good God is to give us His marvelous gifts. To think that each of us, as believers, carries within our own selves the gift or gifts God has individually chosen for us is beyond measure to comprehend. But it is a truth to believe. Often, believers will compare themselves with those that have astounding abilities to be used with their gifts in a public way. They might become discouraged thinking that they could never "match-up" or be used to edify others. Remember the little lady in her bed, using the gift of prayer. As Moody declared, many souls were won by those prayers. Even if she had never been made known to men, God knew, and it was enough.

The gifts are also to be used in love. "In love," just two little words, but what a mighty responsibility they convey. Our gifts are not to be used in self-centered, self-seeking honor, not in haughtiness, not in pride, but in love one to another. The person with the seemingly great gifts and talents must never deem themselves above ministering to the "least" of God's children, for in doing so they serve the Great King of kings. *And the King shall answer and say unto them, Very I say unto you, Inasmuch as ye have done it unto one of the least of these my brethren, ye have done it unto me ... Verily I say unto you, Inasmuch as ye did it not to one of the least of these, ye did it not to me. Matthew 25:40, 45.* We must realize that our gifts and talents are God-given.

We are to be grace dispensers! That is to be one of our titles in life. Mary dispensed grace to the Lord, a grace that was a result of God working in her life. We each can be a grace dispenser to the body of Christ, and to others that need to hear and see the reality of God. We need to give of our gifts and talents to Christ, as surely as Mary poured out all of the ointment that day. *All to Jesus, I surrender, All to Him, I freely give* should be the prayer and song of our hearts. There is a victory in that! A victory for self, for the body of Christ, and for God's honor.

Our gifts are to be cultivated. But first we must understand what gift or gifts we have been given. Job 32:8 says, *There is a spirit in man: and the inspiration of the Almighty giveth them understanding.* God promises to give us understanding of the gifts He gives.

Read John 16:6-13. Apply to spiritual understanding:

Read John 3:27 and comment on how it relates to spiritual gifts.

Read I Timothy 4:6 and 14 and II Timothy 1:6 and tell the challenge to your heart.

It takes a lot of work to cultivate the ground for the planting of seeds and a fruitful harvest. Many a farmer had to learn valuable lessons on that cultivation. We as Christians have hearts that are fertile ground for the planting of God's spiritual gift within. Only God can do that. We cannot conjure up a certain gift, though some may try to imitate it. They will soon find themselves exhausted or discouraged, because only God knows which gift He has chosen for each of us individually. He formed our personalities, potential, and the needs of the body where we are to serve. To consider that unique function we are to have within our community of believers is a responsibility we must not neglect. It is also humbling to know that God formed us for His service.

Read and comment on the following verses about God's forming of each person.

Genesis 2:7-8, 15

Job 33:6

Isaiah 43:7

Isaiah 44:2a

Isaiah 44:24

In Romans Chapter Nine, Paul comments on God's forming of each of us: *Nay but, O man, who art thou that repliest against God? Shall the thing formed say to him that formed it, Why has thou made me thus? Hath not the potter power over the clay... And that he might make known the riches of his glory on the vessels of mercy, which he had afore prepared unto glory. Verses 20-23.* We must not take the negative path of comparing the gifts of others to that which God has formed in us. There is to be a gracious thankfulness that God formed each of us uniquely for His purposes. Only one can take home the Gold Medal in an Olympic race. But that does not mean that others cannot run, or be trainers, or preparers of the tracks. They are all of importance. In speaking of the Christian life, this is why Paul said: *Know ye not that they which run in a race run all, but one receiveth the prize? So run, that ye may obtain. I Corinthians 9:24.* The honor is not just in winning, but in faithfully participating. It is wonderful to see other athletes congratulating the winner of an event that they, too, participated in. It shows their respect and their sportsmanship. We need to encourage one another using honor in preferring one another in love and good Christian "sportsmanship!" It is God's merciful gifting that makes us vessels to be used for His service. All glory is to go to Him!

Just after my third child was born, I had a marvelous ministry to my needs and to my heart. Many had given me gifts before and after the baby came, but the most memorable gift I received came from the sweet Sunday School secretary at our country church. Her name was Susan and I have never forgotten her or her gift. She showed up at my home bright and early when baby was just days old. She smiled a big smile and greeted the older children, boys ages 4 and 6, who had just gotten dressed. She said, "I brought breakfast for you boys." She had checked with my husband the night before and knew the time he went to work. He had told her their favorite breakfast and there it was. She had brought sandwiches, fruit and cookies for their lunch pails and let them help pack up for school. I just marveled. As soon as they had left for the bus, Susan turned to me and said, most quietly and sweetly as was her personality. "Sweet sister, others may be able to sew or are gifted to sing in the choir or play the piano, I cannot do those things. But this one thing I can do, I can clean and care for a home. So today, take time for baby and yourself while I mop floors and vacuum rugs and take the dog for a walk and anything else that needs to be done. And by the way, I brought a casserole that I will leave in the oven with instructions so your husband can reheat it for dinner. A salad and cake will be in the refrigerator." Out the door she went briefly to gather mop bucket and cleaning supplies. What an incredible gift. Not only did it bless me that day and week, but it taught me a deep lesson. The gifts of God are to be used to bless others. Each gift is important. The ministry is important whether it be cleaning the bathrooms at church or arranging the flowers, teaching a Sunday School lesson or gathering up the tally slips of attendance for the church office. All are equally important. Whenever we fail to notice that, we fail God and ourselves. All is to be for His use and His glory. We are to give of what we have been given, our individual talents and gifts, poured out in gratitude and wonder.

Lord,

> *I pour out all that I have,*
> *all that I am,*
> *all that I can be*
> *unto You.*

There are Scriptural examples of God's unique work of shaping each human life in preparation for the use of the gifts given by God's grace:

Apollos:

And a certain Jew named Apollos, born at Alexandria, an eloquent man, and mighty in scriptures, came to Ephesus. This man was instructed in the way of the Lord; and being fervent in spirit, he spake and taught diligently the things of the Lord, knowing only the baptism of John. And he began to speak boldly in the synagogue: whom when Aquila and Priscilla had heard, they took him unto them, and expounded unto him the way of God more perfectly. And when he was disposed to pass unto Achaia, the brethren wrote, exhorting the disciples to receive him: who when he was come, helped them much which had believed through grace: For he mightily convinced the Jews, and that publickly, shewing by the scriptures that Jesus was the Christ. Acts 18:24-28.

God had uniquely formed Apollos, just as He forms each of us, for the gifts and destiny that were planned for him. God had given him talents and abilities to serve Him, even when Apollos did not know that Jesus had already come, died, been buried and rose again. He was a disciple of John the Baptist in the far away Egyptian port city of Alexandria. Think of those that had been prepared there to receive the truth. Surely such a mighty, eloquent speaker for the God given truths of repentance and belief in the One True God, as was Apollos, had been greatly used there. Even in that earlier time,

God was using Apollos. After the events of Acts 18 were carried out, he was prepared to present the great truth of the Gospel. It would have been interesting to view the faces of the prepared vessels in Alexandria, those that were also disciples of John the Baptist's preaching through Apollos, when they too learned that Jesus was the Christ! Perhaps it was by letter from Apollos or a personal messenger, but think of their rejoicing and quick acceptance of the truth. They were as ones for whom the highway of God had truly been prepared.

Think of Aquila and Priscilla, who were where they should be, in the synagogue, when they heard this man Apollos speak with fervor. How their hearts must have burned within as the blessed Holy Spirit spoke eloquently to them to take this man aside, for he was a chosen vessel. They were truly grace dispensers as they shared with Apollos the truth that even John the Baptist had been blessed to know before he died, that Jesus was the Christ, the Lamb of God, the awaited One! Think of the tearful and joyous time they must have spent that day, using their gifts to declare the Glory of God to this prepared man. Oh, what a joy and what a ministry it must have been! Apollos left that day a changed man. He was not shedding the preparation and talents given by God, but gaining redemption and the spiritual gifts given only to the redeemed!

From that day forward, Apollos preached the full Gospel of Jesus Christ! In fact, later the ministry of Apollos is mentioned in equality with that of Paul and Peter, the disciples. Paul, himself, knew the gift of Apollos to the church for its growth and edification:

Who then is Paul, and who is Apollos, but ministers by whom ye believed, even as the Lord gave to every man? I have planted, Apollos watered; but God gave the increase. ... Whether Paul, or Apollos, or Cephas, or the world, or life, or death, or things present, or things to come; all are yours; I Corinthians 3:5-6, 22

And these things, brethren, I have in a figure transferred to myself and to Apollos for your sakes; that ye might learn in us not to think of men above that which is written, that no one of you be puffed up for one against another. I Corinthians 4:6

Paul greatly valued the ministry of Apollos as is evidenced by I Corinthians 16:12: *As touching our brother Apollos, I greatly desired him to come unto you with the brethren...*

Can you think of someone to whom you should express your godly appreciation of their spiritual ministry?

Can you think of some ways that God prepared you before you knew the truth of the Gospel of Jesus Christ?

Dorcas:

Now there was at Joppa a certain disciple named Tabitha, which by interpretation is called Dorcas: this woman was full of good works and alms-deeds which she did. Acts 9:36. Just a "certain" disciple, we might read, yet when she died, all the believers at Joppa mourned. Her simple good works and deeds had so blessed them, that they could not seem to part easily with her. They sent for Peter in Lydda, *desiring that he would not delay to come to them. Then Peter arose and went with them. When he was come, they brought him into the upper chamber* [where Dorcas lay]: *and all the widows stood by him weeping, and shewing the coats and garments which Dorcas made, while she was with them. Acts 9:38-39.* Dorcas' talent seems to have been sewing. God had woven that talent together in an intricate design of beauty with her gifts of compassion and giving. The homely task of garment making had become a thing of ministry in Dorcas' hands. To have so affected the believers there in Joppa, demonstrates how her talents and gifts had graced them all. Perhaps it had even challenged others to use their own gifts to serve. Peter saw their grief and understood through the ministry of the Holy Spirit to his mind that this was a great occasion indeed. *But Peter put them all forth, and kneeled down, and prayed: and turning him to the body said, Tabitha, arise. And she opened her eyes: and when she saw Peter, she sat up. And he gave her his hand, and lifted her up, and when he had called the saints and widows, presented her alive. And it was known throughout all Joppa; and many believed in the Lord. Acts 9:40-42* The talent of sewing reaped many rewards for this dear sister, even into eternity, when it was used for God. She was a grace dispenser.

Are there any abilities that you have that could be used to minister in the practical-spiritual realm to those around you?

Ask God to give you someone to bless this week with the use of your abilities.

David:

"Just a little boy named David" the children's song proclaims. "But he could pray and sing!" The Bible says that David was a man after God's own heart. Even as a young teen, the evidence of David's future faithfulness could be seen: he was entrusted with the care his father's sheep and the performance of duties his father gave to him. The youngest of all the siblings, David was the one who could be counted on to deliver messages even in times of war. The Lord said to Samuel: *I have prepared me a king among [Jesse's] sons. I Samuel 16:1.* David was a prepared vessel, the young boy leading the sheep would one day, as an adult, lead God's people. What a wonder it must have been to Samuel to actually see this *ruddy* youth, *of a beautiful countenance, and goodly to look to. I Samuel 16:12.* Even David's countenance God had prepared, for it would one day bear the countenance of a king. David had the respect of his brothers, as they kept that anointing of Samuel onto the brow of David a cherished secret. Not one of them said in pride, "I am going to be the brother of the king!" There seemed to be an instant awareness of their requirement of loyalty and up holding of this younger brother. Maybe they even stood in complete acknowledgement of God's decision, realizing that "of course it would be David. His heart is so given to God. Have you heard the songs he sings to the sheep as they pasture? They are praises to God!" No wonder that Samuel could anoint David to be the next king *in the midst of this brethren. I Samuel 16:13.* They too were prepared vessels, prepared in loyalty, family structure, bravery and acknowledgement of God's will. Think of how great our God is!

Even before the day of the anointing by Samuel when *the Spirit of the LORD came upon David from that day forward (I Samuel 16:13),* God formed in David prepared talents and abilities. He seemed to love music as evidenced by his harp playing, song writing and dancing. All these would be used in his life in dramatic ways. Being a shepherd from a young age taught him to be watchful and responsible, not just for himself but for the sheep. Later God's people Israel would become David's "flock" to care for. He developed skills of using a sling and stones, staff and rod to protect his sheep, later to be used in the battle with Goliath and many battles for Israel. He was courageous in his defense of the sheep, no matter if it was a lion or a bear that came upon them. He became a courageous youth, leader, general and king. There must have been great strength of body as well as character for David as he led the flock. He doubtless learned the lay of the land, the places of gentle refreshment, even caves of hiding. And all along, David had a prepared heart. When he knelt that day for Samuel's anointing, there did not seem to be any doubts or questions. David was a uniquely prepared young man.

Comment on how David's preparedness is highlighted in these verses: I Samuel 17:32-37, 40-51:

Read I Samuel 17:14-23. Can you think of how David's abilities in music were used to further prepare him to be king one day?

Can you think of a portion of a Psalm written by David that has blessed your life in a special way? Write it here:

Gideon:

What an unusual choice for the theme of this chapter, some might say. But truly there are those that God will use who cannot see the gifts, talents and preparations of the Lord in their lives in order that they might serve Him. One of those types of people was Gideon. He did not realize that he was a prepared vessel at a prepared time to win great victories for God and for the land of Israel. In fact, when we first meet Gideon, in Judges 6:11, he is hiding from the enemy invaders of the land, the Midianites: *And there came an angel of the LORD, and sat under an oak which was in Ophrah, that pertaineth unto Joash the Abiezrite: and his son Gideon threshed wheat by the winepress, to hide it from the Midianites.* The Midianites had invaded and taken over the land of Israel. They had surrounded the land in the time of harvest and taken all that they could, leaving *no sustenance for Israel*, neither crops or animals. Judges 6:3-4. The enemies were so great that the people of Israel saw them as *grasshoppers for multitude ... They entered into the land to destroy it. Judges 6:5-6.* The people of Israel were not only impoverished but they were frightened. The Israelites called out to God to deliver them. Sometimes it takes hardship and loss for God's people to realize their real need, the need for the Lord to move amongst them. The first thing God did in answer to their prayers was to send a prophet into the land to remind the people of God's promises and provisions. We do not even know that prophet's name, just that he was a faithful messenger. It was the message that was important. So, it would be with Gideon as the needed leader. It was not Gideon after all, but the Lord who would deliver His people. God just desired to use a man hiding wheat behind the wine press.

We can assume several things about Gideon and his preparedness. God knew where he was and what he was doing! There is no hiding from God. God had formed him and God had prepared him, even if Gideon did not realize it. He was the youngest of his father's house, he calls himself *the least. Judges 6:15.* Yet he is the one that is threshing the wheat to provide for the family. Even if he was hiding there, it took bravery to even go to thresh the wheat. And if, as some have suggested, the wheat was secretly sown inside the wine press, it also took intelligence to do that. Though in the same verse, he declares that he is not fit to lead Israel, God knew just how fit he actually was. It was perhaps in Gideon's own humility that his qualifications were refined. *And he [Gideon] said unto him, Oh my Lord, wherewith shall I save Israel?...* It was then that God could declare to him: *surely I will be with thee, and thou shalt smite the Midianites as one man. Judges 6:16.* Gideon was a man prepared to realize that any victory had to be of the Lord and not himself. It seems that Gideon had been hiding in God for longer than he had hid the harvest from the enemy. I believe that one of the gifts that God had given Gideon was the gift of knowledge. He had knowledge of the work of God. Another gift was leadership, for as he followed God, others came to join him, in fact, more than were needed for the first job God had for him in battle! Interestingly enough, Gideon also knew how to use a trumpet, for when the men were to be gathered from the land, Judges 6:34 says: *But the Spirit of the LORD came upon Gideon, and he blew a trumpet; and Abiezer was gathered after him.* When Gideon had been assured in knowledge and revelation that his call was from the Lord, he took action. Wise leaders are often required to use a certain ability to pause in consideration of a decision, and then, lead on in action. To act too soon, often puts one in decision by self and not of God. To hesitate in following God's commands can often lead to defeat. Gideon was a prepared vessel after all. His preparation was first and foremost a recognition of and faithfulness to the Lord.

God personally encouraged Gideon after his initial calling of him to service. Read Judges 6:12, 14, 16, 22-23, 39-40. Tell of some of the ways that God encouraged Gideon, even in recognition of Gideon's hesitation and fear:

Can you think of a time that God gave you encouragement to trust Him when all else seemed against you?

Have you ever laid out a fleece to ask God to reassure you of His will in a matter? (Judges 6:36-40). Tell about it:

Some say it is not necessary for Christians to lay out a fleece, that it is doubting God. What do you think?

We must have many thoughts after looking at the lives of some of God's Biblical examples. Remembering that all things are written for our instruction, think on these thoughts:

How does God encourage you to serve Him with the gifts, talents, and abilities He has given you?

Pray about ways you could serve God with the use of that for which He has prepared you:

Look back to the beginning of this chapter and rethink your self-evaluation and see if you want to adjust them here:
What spiritual gift or gifts do you think you have been given?

What do you think are some of your strongest character traits?

What do you think are some of your weakest character traits?

Add a personal prayer to God, referring to the ways He prepared you before you knew Him, gifted you and intertwined your personality and talents:

Pray for your church that the gifts and talents of God will be used to encourage one another, glorify God, and edify the believers:

****

The early morning light softly entered the window of Mary's room.
        The colors of the sunrise
        Were as dancing beams
                Finding their way to her eye lids
                which softly opened to the new day.
In wonder,
Mary's mind came gently awake to the beauty around her.
        "This is the day the Lord hath made,

Let me be happy and rejoice in it, "
Came the whispered prayer
From her lips and the depths of her heart.
She noticed the colors of light beams resting on the Alabaster Box.
It had gleamed in the moon light
And sparkles of the stars
As she had fallen asleep the night before,
Praying that the Lord would give her gentle rest.
Mary marveled
at the placement of that polished box just where it was,
Sitting in her room on a shelf,
To remind her of life and death.
"Lord, is it Your life and death You are reminding me of?
I heard You tell of what You would do,
The time must be near.
What can I do to honor You this day, in my life's deepest service?
I have not Martha's gifts of organization.
I have not Lazarus' gifts of leadership.
What can I give You, Lord?
I would give You my greatest gift,
If I had one to give.
Is it the gift of my heart? I have given You that in devotion already.
Is it the gift of my labors?
I will serve in labor today,
Working next to Martha,
Seeking to serve You as I help her.
What talent, what gift do I have?
"I will give all for you," You whisper to my mind and my heart.
I know it is true,
For You will die,
As the Spotless Lamb of God,
You will give Yourself for me,
In Your death there is love and commitment.
And now I know!

The Alabaster Box,
> *that had gleamed last night, and shines in the morning light,*
>> *It could be a symbol of my heart's devotion,*
>> *It could serve to honor Him who will die.*
> *"Lord, I might not have great talents,*
>> *My gifts may be small, I know,*
>> *But all I am, and all I have, I give to You.*
>>> *Knowing You will give all for me."*

Softly, Mary tiptoed across the room and placed her hands
> *on the Alabaster Box.*
> *It was surely prepared before the time,*
> *To honor the One who was before all time.*
>> *The perfectly smooth surface,*
>> *Assured her of God's perfection.*
>>> *She would break the seal tonight,*
>>> *And pour out all inside,*
>>>> *To honor Him who was her All in all.*

"Lord, know that I will pour out my honor to You this night,
> *In preparation of Your burial,*
> *In knowledge of Your gift,*
>> *You will give soon,*
>> *As You die for our sins.*
>>> *Know my heart, Oh Lord,*
>>> *For my only gift is the gift of my heart.*
>>>> *To You, my Lord and my King."*

Chapter Nine
Give to Him Your Identity

Mark 14:3-9
And being in Bethany in the house of Simon the leper, as he sat at meat,
there came a woman having an alabaster box of ointment of spikenard very precious;
and she brake the box, and poured it on his head.
And there were some that had indignation within themselves, and said,
Why was this waste of the ointment made?
For it might have been sold for more than three hundred pence, and have been given to the poor. And they murmured against her.
And Jesus said, Let her alone; why trouble ye her? She hath wrought a good work on me.
For ye have the poor with you always, and whensoever ye will ye may do them good:
but me ye have not always.
She hath done what she could:
she is come aforehand to anoint my body to the burying.
Verily I say unto you,
Wheresoever this gospel shall be preached throughout the whole world,
this also that she hath done shall be spoken of for a memorial of her.

Mary found her identity in Christ. It is as simple as that, and yet so profound. In our Scripture passage above, she is just called *a woman*. Mary would not slight that identity because of its briefness, but she would have wanted the focus to be on Christ, not on herself. Perhaps there were those at the feast who did not know her, or her relationship to Lazarus. It did not matter. Her identity was in Christ.

She is noted as being one perhaps of wealth, as she brought an expensive *alabaster box of ointment of spikenard very precious.* But it was not a recognition of her wealth that she would have flaunted, but the gift of honor to Christ. After all, at the end of her deed, all had been poured out, given totally to Him. It was not even a recognition of her own intelligence of understanding what Christ would do, as she kept that secret in her heart and spoke not a word. Only Jesus brought up her knowledge of what she was dedicating. She was *come aforehand to anoint my body to the burying,* He had declared. Her act may have been a mystery to the others, but not to Christ. He was the Person she was interested in. Even if her identity was criticized by others, it did not matter. That identity had been swallowed up in devotion to Christ. In Him she found the purpose for her being. Her identity shall always be found as blessed to us who study her life. But at that moment in time, many were seen and heard to murmur against her. Yet her identity to Christ, as part of His spiritual family of believers, was assured. It is why He set up a testimony and memorial for all eternity. He declared, *this also that she hath done shall be spoken of for a memorial of her.* The memorial became part of her identity for all time and eternity, because she had given of herself to Christ.

The question is raised in our own minds: what is my identity? How easy it is to try to find identity in a position. To be head of a committee, officer of an organization or have a title in a company are not our true identities, they are positions in which we are to serve. They are opportunities to witness for Christ by our diligence and trustworthy behavior. But they are not our identity. Do you find your identity in being someone's wife, someone's mother, someone's daughter? Those are God given parts of your legacy and your roles in life, but only your Christian identity can give those roles true meaning. There are many wives, mothers, and daughters, but there are few that live those roles in the power of Christ. Your identity makes a difference! The difference is not only to those around you, but to your own life purpose and goals. What is your identity?

If someone asked you what your identity is, how would you answer?

What are some of the important positions in your life that are honorable?

What are some roles in your life that are life defining?

Are you ever discouraged in any of those positions or roles?

Think of why that may be:

The Scriptures give many descriptive titles and roles to the one who claims Christ as their Savior. The list is long, however, not exhaustive. One who claims the name of Christian, should always remember that they are carrying around the very presence of Christ where ever they go and whatever they do. Mary is known in the memorials of Heaven, as one who honored Christ. There is no higher identity that we can claim!

Read the following descriptive titles of a Christian, along with a related Scripture verse, and remark on each one and how it applies to you:

Saint (Romans 1:7):

Child of God (Romans 8:16):

Ambassador (II Corinthians 5:20):

Christ in You (Colossians 1:27):

Servant of Christ (Romans 6:22):

Fellow Laborer (I Corinthians 3:9):

Fruitbearer (Colossians 1:10):

Part of the Beloved Brethren (I Corinthians 15:58):

Heir (Romans 8:17):

Vessel of Honor (II Timothy 2:21):

Vessel of Mercy (Romans 9:23):

Witness (Acts 1:8):

There is an amazing title of identity that we might sometimes take casually, but it is all encompassing: Christian. Read the following verses and comment on how it magnifies the identity of the title of Christian in your mind:

Acts 11:26:

Hebrews 9:2:

I Peter 4:16:

What do you feel are your responsibilities as a Christian?

Can you think of places in the world today where claiming the identity as "Christian" brings great danger to the believer?

How does it humble you to think of your life, compared to Christians in other lands where they do not have the freedoms we have?

How does it challenge you?

Have you ever had your identity as a Christian criticized or threatened?

How would you explain the real meaning of "Christian" to someone who thinks they are a Christian because of their heritage, church membership or national residence?

Always, we need to consider how our other identities with the world can be encompassed with our identity as Christians. Think of how that would alter the actions, attitudes and deeds of some Christians with the following identities:

Christian Who Is A Legislator:

Christian Who Is A Store Owner:

Christian Who Is A Company Owner:

Christian Who Is A Salesperson:

Christian Who Is A Parent:

Christian Who Is A Wife:

Christian Who Is A Daughter:

Christian Who Is A Worker in Industry:

Christian Who Is A School Teacher:

Christian Who Is A Military Personnel:

Christian Who Is A Housewife:

Christian Who Is A Friend:

Christian Who Is A Sibling:

Christian Who Is An Athlete:

Christian Who Is A Musician:

Christian Who Is An Artist:

Christian Who Is A Writer:

Are there any ways that putting the title "Christian" in front of one of your identity titles could affect your life decisions?

Think of some of your title identities and place the name Christian in front of them. How will that effect how you live this week?

Being a Christian also involves titles and identities as the result of our salvation. Redeemed, Righteous, Forgiven, Justified. All these have to do with believing in the death, burial and resurrection of Christ, of believing that His shed blood covered all our sins.

Read the verses noted after each Christian "Title" from the paragraph above. Then write your own definition of the word of the title:

Redeemed: Revelation 5:9

Righteous: Colossians 1:11, Colossians 2:15, Philippians 3:9

Forgiven: Psalm 103:10-11, Psalm 85:2

Justified: Romans 5:1, I Corinthians 6:11

Are you secure in your identity as being among the Redeemed, Righteous, Forgiven and Justified?

Can you tell the date of your being born again into God's Forever Kingdom and receiving those new identities?

In realizing our identity with Christ, there should be many overwhelming feelings that dwell with us. Comment on those below:

Gratitude (Colossians 1:12):

Love (I Peter 1:8):

Desire to Honor Christ (Isaiah 25:1):

Praise to Christ (Hebrews 13:15)

Add to this list additional personal feelings you have concerning your identity in Christ:

Knowing our identity with Christ, should cause us to give of our person to Him for whatever He chooses. It is our "Person" that He is most interested in. Some have said: "I am not a good singer, so I can't serve Christ," "I am too old to clean the church, I can't serve there," "I do not have much money, I can't serve in that way." Instead, we should realize that it is our hearts that Christ wants to be given to Him. He wants us to trust Him with our identity, all of who we are. At our own memorial service will others just say, "she was a nice woman," "she could bake the best pies," "she had a beautiful singing voice." All those are good things and part of our uniqueness, but our Christian identity should be remembered. What an honor for those that knew us to first say, "she was a dedicated and loving Christian woman." That is our good reward of man – to be seen as totally in Jesus!

Oh, Lord,
I bow my head in awe at that which You have given to me,
A new identity,
All because of Your love and sacrifice.
Help me to live every day as a Daughter of the King!

****

But ye are a chosen generation, a royal priesthood, an holy nation, a peculiar people;
That ye should show forth the praises of him
who called you out of darkness into his marvellous light:
I Peter 2:9

****

Just like the oil that Mary poured out, we are to be poured out, given totally to Christ. The oil was a costly item, but each of us is costlier. It took the precious blood of Christ to purchase our redemption! He gladly paid it, for you and for me. Let us be given totally on the altar of devotion to Christ. Even if we are "poured out" and "used up" for Him. Our identity is sure, it is secure, it is in Christ!

Broken and Spilled Out *Written by: Bill George, Gloria Gaither*

One day a plain village woman, Driven by love for her Lord Recklessly poured out a valuable essence, Disregarding the scorn.
And once it was broken and spilled out, A fragrance filled all the room,
Like a pris'ner released from his shackles, Like a spirit set free from the tomb.

Lord, You were God's precious treasure, His loved and His own perfect Son,
Sent here to show me, The love of the Father,
Just for love it was done.

And though You were perfect and holy,

You gave up Yourself willingly,

You spared no expense for my pardon
You were used up and wasted for me.

Broken and spilled out, Just for love of me Jesus
God's most precious treasure, Lavished on me,
You were broken and spilled out, And poured at my feet,
In sweet abandon, Lord, You were spilled out and used up for
Me.

Broken and spilled out, Just for love of you, Jesus
My most precious treasure, Lavished on Thee,
Broken and spilled out, And poured at Your feet,
In sweet abandon, Let me be spilled out And used up for
Thee.

Lord, let us find our identity in You.

****

Martha had watched her sister Mary all day.
When they left their house that morning,
Bound for the preparation for the feast,
Mary had been quiet,
Carrying a bundle close to her heart.
In the rooms of preparation, Martha saw that Mary was busy,
Diligent in the work needing to be done,
Encouraging in her sisterly looks and help.
Mary had been quiet,
As if she carried a burden close to her heart.
In the rush of the last minute duties, Mary's hands had not been idle,
They had continued to stir the food
Simmering in large pots.

Mary had been quiet,
*   As if the quiet was held tightly in her heart.*
Now the food had been served, and Martha was grateful
*   For the actions of her sister*
*   Whom she embraced with her eyes.*
*   But Mary was quiet still,*
*   Looking as if she had a charge of heart to do.*
Martha quietly followed as Mary departed the room
*   Into the courtyard outside,*
*   There to retrieve her shawl and bundle.*
*   The air all around was quiet,*
*   As if holding its breath for Mary's heart journey.*
It only took a few steps for Mary to stand at the doorway,
*   Of the room where the men were eating,*
*   Of the room where dear Jesus was discoursing.*
*   On quiet feet Mary walked behind Him,*
*   Took out a shining box from her bundle,*
*   And broke the seal in one movement.*
*   Then poured out the oil with devotion of heart.*
Martha watched in quiet awe as her sister silently continued her act.
*   The oil covered Jesus's head*
*   And ran down His body onto His feet.*
*   Quiet Mary did not hesitate,*
*   No matter what others said,*
*   It did not seem to wound her heart.*
*   All she seemed to see was Jesus*
*   And the oil as it flowed in a stream.*
At first Martha had thought to draw her sister back from the room,
*   But her awe joined with the fragrance*
*   Of the oil of ointment prepared for burials.*
*   Then Jesus spoke, and she understood,*
*   This was the burden Mary had carried close all day.*
A soft smile crossed Martha's lips as she looked

At her sister and she knew,
As Jesus said, Mary had done this ahead of time
To anoint Him for His soon and coming burial.
Of which they had spoken sister heart to sister heart.
Indeed, Mary had chosen the better part again that day,
In her quiet way she had come,
To do what she could
To show her devotion and understanding,
Of the work of the Savior who had won their hearts.
Martha waited for her sister at the doorway,
As she did, she prayed,
With tears streaming down her face.
Thank You, God, for this sister,
Who so deeply understands that which Your Son will do
When He dies for us,
So our hearts can be cleansed and pure.
The contention in the room had been quieted,
As Jesus had rebuked the scorners,
And praised that which He said was her memorial.
Mary's graceful hands finished their work,
The pieces were gathered and she departed the room.
That day Mary had shown the love in her heart.
As she gave honor to the Savior.
The fragrance and the stillness lingered,
As Mary came out and into Martha's embrace.
Their hearts were entwined as one.

Chapter Ten
Giving of Myself to God

Is Your All on the Altar?

You have longed for sweet peace, and for faith to increase,
And have earnestly, fervently prayed;
But you cannot have rest or be perfectly blest
Until all on the altar is laid.

Is your all on the altar of sacrifice laid?
Your heart, does the Spirit control?
You can only be blest and have peace and sweet rest,
As you yield Him your body and soul.

O we never can know what the Lord will bestow
Of the blessings for which we have prayed.
Till our body and soul He doth fully control,
And our all on the altar is laid.

Is your all on the altar of sacrifice laid?
Your heart, does the Spirit control?
You can only be blest and have peace and sweet rest,
As you yield Him your body and soul.

Elisha A. Hoffman

****

I beseech you therefore, brethren, by the mercies of God,
That ye present your bodies a living sacrifice,
Holy, acceptable unto God,
Which is your reasonable service.
Romans 12:1

****

In this chapter, we will consider the ultimate giving to God, the giving of ourselves. Individually, we must make the decision to give all to the Lord, pictured as laying ourselves on the altar of commitment.

It is often easy to talk about what we should give to God. We have considered thinking of whether we should give that hour of time each week to work with the children at church. Perhaps, we should give that special offering for missions and forgo that new dress. Or maybe we need to give a gift to help a charitable need. But what about giving of ourselves. All of who we are. All of who we can be. In essence, that is what the woman with the Alabaster Box did that day long ago. She gave all of herself to Jesus. She let go of ambition, timidity, treasure, reputation and much more. It was poured out with the oil from the Alabaster Box. Totally. It does not seem that she measured out a portion of the oil. Neither did she lift the container away until there was no more oil flowing. She gave it totally. And that is what we must do with our own lives, give them totally to the Lord, holding nothing back.

Pagans in the time of Biblical writing saw sacrifice in a different way. They often passed their children through the fires lit on the sacrificial altar. They would cut themselves and offer sacrifices of wailing and prostrating themselves before an idol. All those ways are repugnant to us. The reason they are so contrary to true Christian sacrifice of self, is that they bring disgrace. True Biblical giving of self is a devotion of beauty and commitment of all we are to the God who sent the Only True Sacrifice, His Son Jesus

Christ. The sacrifice of Christ was a one-time occurring event: the Crucifixion on Calvary's Hill. This ultimate sacrifice was given with eternity's values in mind. It was the Gift of God on the altar of sacrifice for us. It has everlasting results. To try to add anything to that sacrifice would be a purposeful affront to the Almighty God and to our Savior, Jesus Christ.

The giving of ourselves is not an addition or a substitute for believing in the one-time sacrifice of Christ. Instead, it is an honoring of what He has done for us. It is our mind, body and soul dedicated with purpose in a thanksgiving praise to God. It is like saying, "Lord, You have given all for me. Take all that I am in praise and thanksgiving for that great love. Use me in the way You choose. Fix my feet solidly on Your path of life for me. Let me arise from this point of commitment, to live for You every day of my life."

In such a self-giving, there is honor. At the point of salvation, one becomes as a recruit in the Lord's army. With the giving of self, one becomes a well-trained soldier in that army, ready for marching orders. We can with pride hold the banner high that proclaims the name of our Lord. We are under His command and the battles are not wholly ours anymore. We are in the Lord's army and He is our Commander and the Captain that leads us. We can only follow when we are in that place of total commitment.

There was a revival begun under the reign of King Hezekiah in Judah. The verses that conclude the amazing description of that time of restoration to true worship, involve the real impact of revival on the lives of God's people in total commitment.

In speaking of the Levites, it is said: *...through all the congregation: for in their set office they sanctified themselves in holiness. II Chronicles 31:18b.* How would you define the phrase *sanctified themselves in holiness?*

Why do you think this phrase is a good summary of how to serve and to seek God?

As a testimony to all of Israel, the king stood forth for total commitment to God. Read II Chronicles 31:20-21. How did Hezekiah demonstrate the "formula" for total dedication to God?

How do you think the people that observed Hezekiah's devotion reacted?

There are some interesting Hebrew words used in this section of Scripture in relation to what Hezekiah did. Read the Hebrew meanings of these direct English words and comment on them:

Good: excellent, agreeable:

Right: straight, upright, correct, just:

Truth: faithful, firm, sure, reliable:

Prospered: advance, succeed, be made profitable, to "come mightily":

When Hezekiah began the cleansing of God's house and the restoration of true worship in Judah, there is a very vivid description of the first worship services found in II Chronicles 29:28-31. What actions stand out to you in this description?

Read II Chronicles 29:36 and tell the end result that day:

What do you think the phrase, *upright in heart,* found in verse 34 of the chapter, means?

How does that apply to our commitment to God?

One of the more consuming thoughts of my recent meditations has been the difference between <u>all</u> and <u>segments</u> of the all. God does not want us to have a segmented life! That is one where we pick and choose which parts of our lives are to be given over in dedication to God and which parts we would want to keep for ourselves. It does not work. In a previous devotional book, *Lessons From Ladies Of Faith*, I used the illustration of the sections of an orange. What happens in each segment of that orange affects the whole. The whole is made up of a complete joining of the segments. The membranes between each segment are thin, almost transparent. If there is rottenness in one segment, the entire orange is affected. Left on the counter, it will soon completely rot. Cut apart, the taste of what looked to be healthy segments will be affected by the one that is not. There is a transparency in our lives between segmentations of our whole. We cannot think that what is done in one segment will not affect the others. In fact, in real life, the segment divisions seem to disappear. Whether this is because of the effect of sin and bad choices in what we thought were isolated sections, or what happens in a truly totally committed life for God, the transfer is real. We cannot avoid it: the whole is truly become an "all" in the living of our lives. Each area of our life is important to God. We cannot be like Hezekiah and prosper, unless each segment is consecrated to God.

In the study of the giving of ourselves totally to God, there are certain key concepts that are involved. Read the verses listed below concerning some of these concepts. Comment on any of the verses and how they relate to your life.

Consecration:
For Moses had said, Consecrate yourselves to day to the LORD... that he may bestow upon you a blessing this day. Exodus 32:29

I beseech you therefore, brethren, by the mercies of God, that ye present your bodies a living sacrifice, holy, acceptable unto God, which is your reasonable service. Romans 12:1

The very God of peace sanctify you wholly; and I pray God your whole spirit and soul and body be preserved blameless unto the coming of our Lord Jesus Christ. I Thessalonians 5:23

The deeper life:
For ye are bought with a price: therefore glorify God in your body, and in your spirit, which are God's. I Corinthians 6:20

Hereby perceive we the love of God, because he laid down his life for us: and we ought to lay down our lives for the brethren. I John 3:16

Sacrifices of praise:
And let them sacrifice the sacrifices of thanksgiving and declare his works with rejoicing. Psalm 107:22

By him therefore let us offer the sacrifice of praise to God continually, that is, the fruit of our lips giving thanks to his name. Hebrews 13:15

Spiritual resurrection:

And you hath he quickened, who were dead in trespasses and sins; And hath raised us up together, and made us sit together in heavenly places in Christ Jesus. Ephesians 2:1, 6

If ye then be risen with Christ, seek those things which are above, where Christ sitteth on the right hand of God. Colossians 3:1

Reverence:

Stand in awe, and sin not... Psalm 4:4

God is greatly to be feared in the assembly of the saints, and to be had in reverence of all them that are about him. Psalm 89:7

Sanctification:

If any man therefore purge himself from these [sins]*, he shall be a vessel unto honour, sanctified, and meet for the master's use, and prepared unto every good work. II Timothy 2:21*

Sanctify them through thy truth: thy word is truth. John 17:17

Self-Denial:

Then said Jesus unto his disciples, If any man will come after me, let him deny himself, and take up his cross, and follow me. Matthew 16:24

For if ye live after the flesh, ye shall die: but if ye through the Spirit do mortify the deeds of the body, ye shall live. Romans 8:13

Yea doubtless, and I count all things but loss for the excellency of the knowledge of Christ Jesus my Lord: for whom I have suffered the loss of all things, and do count them but dung, that I may win Christ. Philippians 3:8

Abiding in Christ:

He that saith he abideth in him ought himself also so to walk, even as he walked. I John 2:6

Servants of Christ:

Labor not for the meat which perisheth, but for that meat which endureth unto everlasting life, which the Son of man shall give unto you: for him hath God the Father sealed. John 6:27

If any man serve me [Jesus], let him follow me; and where I am, there shall also my servant be: if any man serve me, him will my Father honour. John 12:26

There is a certain profound humility that must be in all who totally give of themselves to God. There can be no boasting in spirituality. One is not to think of themselves as being more spiritual because of what he has done. Our condition of spirit is all of Christ. How can we even compare ourselves to our spotless Lamb of Glory, our Savior Jesus Christ, and not be humbled within. All that we are, and all that we can be, should belong to Him. The vanity of earthly life is spoken of by Peter: *For all flesh is as grass, and all the glory of man as the flower of grass. The grass withereth, and the flower thereof falleth away: But the word of the Lord endureth for ever. And this is the word which by the gospel is preach unto you. I Peter 1:24-25.* Therefore, let us give of our selves totally to God who will lift us up to be with Him in Heavenly places. We must be eternally minded to have victory in the Christian life.

To fall on the altar of love for God, is to proclaim with Isaiah: *O LORD, thou art my God; I will exalt thee, I will praise thy name; for thou hast done wonderful things; thy counsels of old are faithfulness and truth. Isaiah 25:1*

How does this verse affect your commitment to God?

There are three examples that come readily to mind of people in the Bible that gave themselves totally to God. Let us study the commitments of these, and relate them to our own lives.

Esther:

Esther was a captive Jewish orphan in Babylon. She was being raised by her cousin after the death of her parents. We do not know how old she was when her cousin Mordecai became her guardian, but we do know that Mordecai was a Jewish man of great commitment to God. He would have raised Esther to know the commandments of the Lord. She would have known God's desire for the chosen people of Israel to worship God alone and also for young maidens to marry a Jewish man. Yet, Esther was a captive. Some of her decisions would soon be taken from her, but we find that she never forsook the Lord in her heart.

The first dramatic thing we see in Scripture that happened to Esther was the result of a "contest" to find King Ahasuerus' next wife. In every province of the land of the Persians and the Medes, the governors of the land were to choose the most beautiful maidens to be brought to the palace of the king. Esther is described in Esther 2:7 as *fair and beautiful.* The governor of her province saw her beauty and chose her to send to the palace.

How do you suppose most of the young women felt who were chosen for the contest?

How do you think Esther felt?

Her cousin Mordecai had *charged her (Esther 2:10)* that she not reveal her Jewish heritage, and she had obeyed. Why do you think she had to do this?

Even though Esther kept her promise not to tell that she was Jewish, in what ways do we know she continued to live for the Lord?

Read Esther 2:9:

Read Esther 2:15: (Hint – she did not rely on any ornate or alluring dress, she trusted the person given in authority over her)

Great danger was placed on all the Jews of the land by an order to have them killed on a certain day. Mordecai sent a message to Esther:

Read Esther 4:13-14. What was asked of Esther?

How did this require her to make a decision to give herself totally to God?

Read Esther 4:15-16. What was her decision?

What phrase tells that she totally placed her life in God's hands?

Have you ever thought of the depth of giving your entire life unto God, even if that results in death?

The rest of the story is told through the remainder of the Book of Esther. God greatly rewarded Esther's choice of total commitment whether in life or death. Her people, the Jews, were saved. She was spared and commended of the king. Her beloved Mordecai was given honor. Even the enemy of the Jews was destroyed. All this happened because one captive Jewish maiden was willing to place her entire life in God's hands.

Comment on these key elements in Esther's decision and how they relate to our lives:
Prayer:

Laying her life totally on God's spiritual altar:

Living a consistent godly life showing God's grace to others:

The remembrance of the victory won because of Esther's bravery, faithfulness and commitment is recorded in Scripture in the establishment of a yearly memorial for the Jews, even to this day:
As the days wherein the Jews rested from their enemies,
And the month which was turned unto them from sorrow to joy,
And from mourning into a good day:
That they should make them days of feasting and joy,
And of sending portions one to another,
And of gifts to the poor.
Esther 9:22

Josiah:

Near the end of the Books of II Kings and II Chronicles, we read of the last kings of the Davidic line to rule in Judah before the captivity. Constantly, from the days of the son of Solomon, we read of kings that honored the Lord and those that went away from the Lord. It seems so strange to us to think that those living in the promised land, who had the temple of the Lord in Jerusalem, and had a heritage of knowing the way of the Lord and even the teachings of David and Solomon, would so completely turn from the truth of the Lord God. But many did. The people of the land most often followed the example of their kings.

What a tremendous responsibility that should lay on our hearts concerning the witness of our testimony of the Lord in the positions that God has placed us. Each of us has a position of influence, whether it be with our children at home, with our husband, our family or in a corporation or even politics. Whether we are given totally to the Lord or not, the example will be given. Our accountability is great. Our influence may seem small, but as with ripples in a pond, they ever reach into wider and wider circles of impact. We should take heed from the history of the kings of Judah. No matter how often we have heard the Scriptures or how often we have gone to church, the value of our life will be apparent for all to see. God is a God of truth and His truth cannot be hidden. We have a constant choice whether to live for the Lord or for the things of the world, and others are watching!

Josiah was a good king who reigned for thirty-one years. *And he did that which was right in the sight of the Lord, and walked in the ways of David his father, and declined neither to the right hand, nor to the left. II Chronicles 34:2.*

The Hebrew word for *decline* means departed or turned aside. How dynamic is the statement that Josiah declined neither to the right hand, nor to the left?

Read II Chronicles 34:3 and comment on what you learn about Josiah there.

Josiah ruled as king in Judah after the reign of his father Amon, who was so evil that the Bible says he *trespassed more and more.* Because of this, his servants killed him and then the people of the land killed those servants. What a time to take over the throne and, doubly so, at such a young age as Josiah. It is interesting that Josiah's grandfather Manasseh had been a king that had done evil also. God warned Manasseh and the people of the land of this evil, and yet they would not turn from their sins. *Wherefore the LORD brought upon them the captains of the host of the king of Assyria, which took Manasseh among the thorns, and bound him with fetters, and carried him away to Babylon.* It would seem the story of Josiah's grandfather would end there, in disgrace or even death. But the story continues.

Read II Chronicles 33:12-13. Comment on the following words found in the verses:
    Besought:

    Humbled:

    Greatly:

    Then Manasseh knew that the LORD he was God:

Josiah was only eight years old when he began to reign as king. His father Amon had only reigned two years after the death of Manasseh. Do you think it is possible that a very young Josiah, perhaps five or six years old, could have sat with his grandfather and had Manasseh tell him of the necessity to make a total commitment to God?

We have found that Josiah was *yet young* when he began to seek after the Lord. How important is it to train up a child from his earliest years to know about the reality of God?

We do not know of the relationship of Josiah with his grandfather, or of the stories he may have heard of his godly great grandfather, Hezekiah, but at a time of great spiritual need, this very young boy made amazing decisions to live totally for the Lord. He also knew the importance of leading the people of Judah to worship God in the correct way. Think of it, he had lived through the murder of his own father by servants. Following that, there seems to have been a rebellion of a good sort, but a rebellion none the less. Josiah at age eight seems to have been a very brave and focused individual.

No matter the history of kingly murders, he was going to take a bold stand. He was going to totally give his life to the Lord and encourage others to do the same! It often takes a great courage of heart to make a faithful stand. As with Esther's account, in his young mind, Josiah may have realized, "If I perish, I perish, but I have decided that to live is to live unto God."

I, for one, stand amazed at the courage of this young boy. His life story only gets more impressive spiritually as he grows older. At twenty, perhaps when he had no assistant in reigning, he started to give the orders to totally cleanse Judah and Jerusalem from all false idols and worship. At age 26, he began to work with his governors and the priests to cleanse the house of the Lord in Jerusalem. It was a mighty task, from putting in new flooring to repairing all the temple. In II Chronicles 34:12, it is told that the workers did the work *faithfully*.

What is the impact of the word *faithfully* to living for the Lord and doing the jobs He gives you to do?

In the repair of the temple, the Scriptures, or the "Book," was found that had been neglected. It was brought before Josiah and read to him. He was almost overwhelmed with grief, realizing all the years that the people had not lived for the Lord. His heart was broken, wanting the people of the land to know the words of the book.

How does this remind you of our responsibility to tell the truth of the Scriptures to others?

Read II Chronicles 34:26-28. What was the message God sent to Josiah?

Why do you think it is important to have a tender heart?

Josiah called all the leaders of Judah together to Jerusalem. There he personally read to them the *words of the book of the covenant*. Notice that this young king did not leave the "job" to others, but personally did it himself. What a reminder this is to us that we cannot leave the reading and teaching of God's Word just to others, even to our godly pastors. God gives each of us the responsibility to share His Word.

Read II Corinthians 5:20. Paul tells us that we are ambassadors for Christ. Remembering the example of Josiah, what do you think this position involves?

Read II Chronicles 34:30-33. They are the last verses in this chapter about Josiah. What things did you learn from these verses?

When Josiah made his covenant before the LORD and all the people, it says he made certain promises. What were they?

How did he purpose to follow his promises?

Did you notice the totality of his commitment! There was no segmented part of Josiah's life. He gave it all! In the King James Bible, it says that Josiah caused all that were present *to stand to it!* The Hebrew meaning of that phrase is very strong. It includes the ideas of taking a stand for what is right and holding one's ground, no matter what! Further, it can mean to stand firm and maintain that stand.

How important in the giving of one's life to God, is the phrase *to stand to it*?

Re-read the final verse, verse thirty-three, and tell how long Josiah kept his commitment to God:

Are you willing to pray the commitment of Josiah and ask God to help you not to depart, ever in your life, from following Christ? Write a prayer for yourself here, relate it to all you have learned of Josiah's faithfulness to God:

Daniel:

Daniel also was a captive from the land of Judah taken by the armies of Nebuchadnezzar, king of Babylon. The king directed the gathering of *the children of Israel, and of the king's seed, and of the princes; Children in whom was no blemish, but well favored, and skillful in wisdom, and cunning in knowledge, and understanding science, and as such as ability in them to stand in the king's palace, and whom they might teach the learning and the tongue of the Chaldeans. Daniel 1:3-4* Daniel was one of those chosen ones. He may even have been a prince of Judah. This we do know, he was a young person whose life was totally saturated with commitment to the Lord God of Israel. No matter if he was in a foreign land, no matter if he was being groomed to be a well- educated vassal of Babylon, no matter that he had been separated from the rest of the captives, Daniel was a young man whose life was given to God.

Again, we see the courage of commitment in Daniel's life. The king, who had the power of life and death over his captives, who also had made the rules for those continuing in the special education program, had given commandment over every aspect of their lives.

Even the food they were to eat was appointed. There would have been great danger in not obeying the king. Yet, Daniel knew he had to obey God rather than men! (Acts 5:29) Under Old Testament law, Daniel would have been disobeying God if he had eaten the food and wine ordered for him and his companions. A very strong word is used in reference to Daniel's brave decision: *defile*. To have obeyed the king in this somewhat "small" matter would have been to cause himself to be defiled! In Hebrew, the word defile has the meaning of pollute, stain or desecrate. Desecrate is a dynamic word in English! It is a violent disrespect and a violation of that which is good! What some of the other young Jewish youths might have thought they could justify because of their captive state, Daniel saw as a decision point. In essence, he was saying the same as Esther, "If I perish, I perish."

The amazing thing is that Daniel had such total trust in God, that he said to the overseers: *prove thy servants. Daniel 1:12* With commitment comes trust. The image of a child nestling close to his mother, shows total trust, total commitment. That is the reality of how we should be with our Lord, drawing closer and closer, pressed to His heart, totally trusting, totally committed. Daniel was like that! His entire destiny was determined by the proof of Daniel and his three friends that could only be made by the Lord. Instead of eating the food, meat and wine of the Babylonians, they asked for just vegetables and water. Totally, the four youths laid their bodies on the altar of faith. God demonstrated in power and personal intimacy with the youths, the importance of faithfulness to Him. No matter what, no matter where, God is to be obeyed. The proof was in the physical health and strength of the youths, and in the fact that they excelled in all mental tests and demonstrations of wisdom! Only God could do that.

When the chosen Jewish youths are described, they are seen to be handsome, physically excellent, intelligent and of the greatest ability.

How could that have caused some to value self instead of God?

Do you think that some of the youths in the program felt privileged and above their brethren?

How significant is it that we only know the names of the four who decided to take a stand for God?

What could have been the consequences of challenging the rulings?

Can you think of some ways when you might be called upon to "refuse" to defile yourself with worldly things?

What difference does it make whether we go along with our peers or separate ourselves for God?

Do you think the other youths may have mocked Daniel and his friends?

Read Daniel 1:19. Did you notice that the names of the four listed there are all their Jewish names? How does this speak to you about their identity in God?

How does that remind you that God knows you personally?

Daniel continued to stand for the Lord God, even when he was put into a place of leadership and honor. He did this under more than one king and in many situations. It also seems evident that he worked hard and fulfilled his earthly responsibilities given by the kings.

How important is it to be seen as a diligent worker in our employment or household as a testimony of our commitment to God?

Do you think the world looks for ways to criticize Christians who have taken a stand for God?

How hard is it to be seen as "different" in our present world?

One of the recorded deeds of Daniel is found in Daniel chapter two. There Daniel gives an interpretation of a dream that had deeply bothered the king. The king had given a command that all of the wise men should seek to learn the meaning of the dream. This command contained the very real threat of death if a lie was told, but of reward if the truth was made known. The Chaldean sorcerers were greatly afraid. They asked the king to take back the command.

Read Daniel 2:12-13. What was the king's reaction to the request of the false wisemen?

Daniel and his fellows were included in the death order. They were counted as among the wise men of the land. How easily is it to be "lumped together" with all who have a certain position or profession? (hint: "all" teachers, "all" women, "all" politicians)

Read Daniel 2:14-18. What was Daniel's response to this sentence of death?

How important was prayer in his course?

Read Daniel 2:19-23. This is a beautiful and very personal prayer of praise and thanksgiving. How important to your understanding of the life commitment of Daniel is it to know that he took time to pray to God before he told the king the meaning of the dream?

Imagine the bravery of Daniel as he marched into the palace that day, the last day of the reprieve from the death sentence. Quietly examine your heart and consider if there is anything that would cause you to hesitate to take a stand for Christ?

To see the results of the meeting, read Daniel 2:47-49. Daniel and his friends were taken from the sentence of death to positions of great favor. Does this always happen when we take a stand for Christ?

Should the end result before the world make any difference in our commitments?

There are more instances of Daniel's bravery told in the rest of the Book of Daniel. Take time to read these for yourself. It will bless your heart. Even his three friends took courageous stands for the Lord. Twice, these four men were willing to lay their lives on the literal altar of death instead of defiling their commitment to God.

There is a wonder of strength of character in a person who has totally given their life to the Lord. The real wonder is when we consider that this strength of character can be ours as we continue to lay our lives on the altar of total abandonment unto God.

What are some of the things you think modern day Christians might have to abandon for God?

What do you think it means to be abandoned <u>unto</u> God?

In summing up the life of Daniel, the Scriptures declare: *So this Daniel prospered in the reign of Darius, and in the reign of Cyrus the Persian. Daniel 6:28.* In what ways would you want to "prosper" in your life?

God makes a beautiful promise to Daniel:
>*But go thy way till the end be: for thou shalt rest,*
>*and stand in thy lot at the end of the days.*
>*Daniel 12:13*

Comment on this promise and how it might relate to your life:

All three of our examples were real people. Though they were each in unique positions in life, so are each of us. We all have positions of influence. Those positions can be seen as being lived for the world and self, or for God. There is a profound difference between the two styles of life. God gives us the choice. We stand before figurative doors to a fiery furnace. Satan seeks to devour us as a lion would his prey. Yet there is the choice of entering into a powerful intimate relationship with our holy God. Christ calls to us:

Whosoever will come after me, let him deny himself,
and take up his cross, and follow me.
Mark 8:34

There is great victory in abandoning our own narrow view of life and, instead, following closely to Christ. May we have the courage to deny ourselves, take up our crosses of commitment, and follow Jesus all the way down life's pathway. At the end there will be a reward of great joy.

****

Yesterday, there had been a hush around the house,
    As if it was waiting,
        Waiting for something important,
           something new.
Early in the morning, the hush disappeared,
    There was an excitement in the air,
        Excitement for something important,
           something new.
                Jesus was coming!
Mary's heart beat faster with anticipation,
    The Master would be here,
        She anticipated the importance,
           prayed for what would be heard!
She had heard Him teach before,
    And her heart had been stirred,
        Deep feelings had awakened
        Within.
She thought silently, I can not miss a word Jesus says,
    I will stay close by this time,
        He could whisper and I will hear it.
        He is coming!
The house started to fill with neighbors and others she did not know,

But there was only One that she looked for,
It was the Master and He was at the door.
"Let Him in!"
She called to another.
Martha called to her from the place of preparation,
"How many are there, Mary"
Oh, but Mary only wanted to see One.
Her mind was now set,
She had to know Him better.
Quickly Mary counted those gathered around the place the Master chose,
"There are so many, Martha.
Do not worry,
The Master has come."
He began to speak, and all the noise hushed around Him,
On velvet footsteps, Mary came,
To sit at His feet,
To hear His words,
To know more of Him.
All around her seemed to fade away,
The others, the noise, the work to do,
There was only Jesus,
And here she would stay,
There was naught else she could do.
She had chosen.
Quietly the words of Jesus came from into her ears,
and into her mind,
and then into her heart.
His message is my something new!
His teaching is important.
She felt the excitement within.
And then she knew.
She had to really listen,

Because she heard a whisper as within her heart,
Even as Jesus continued to speak clearly,
To those gathered around,
The whisper came.
"Let me in, Mary," it softly said,
"Make Me your focus," it continued,
"Learn more of Me," came the invitation.
There on the floor, sitting at His feet, Mary responded,
In her mind and in her heart,
She said, "Yes!
Lord, come into my heart,
Make my focus set on You,
Teach me more each day!"
For just an instant, Jesus cast His eyes on her,
Despite the crowd, He knew!
Softly He smiled as He kept teaching,
But the smile let her know.
He had come into her heart,
He had sharpened her focus,
He would teach her anew!
Jesus had come,
and Mary's life was complete.

****

Oh, how great is thy goodness,
which thou hast laid up for them that fear thee;
Which thou hast wrought for them that trust in thee...
Psalm 31:19

Chapter Eleven
Give of Your Self as a Woman

For thy Maker is thine husband;
The LORD of host is his name;
And thy Redeemer the Holy One of Israel;
The God of the whole earth shall he be called.

The LORD hath called thee as a woman....
...my kindness shall not depart from thee,
neither shall the covenant of my peace be removed,
saith the LORD that hath mercy on thee.
....
Behold, I will lay thy stones with fair colors,
and lay thy foundations with sapphires.
And I will make thy windows of agates, and thy gates of carbuncles,
and all thy borders of pleasant stones.
Isaiah 54:5-12   Selected

The selected verses from Isaiah paint a beautiful picture. It is as if God, Himself, has built a cottage for the woman. God's cottage is no ordinary cottage, it has foundations of sapphires, windows of agate and borders of pleasant stones. The image of this place is all of peace and quiet joy. Surely there is a quiet stream flowing by, trees with lovely song birds and the gentle filtering of the sun onto the path of fair colors. It is true that this section of Scripture has more to say. It was written for a woman *forsaken and grieved in spirit, and a wife of youth, when thou wast refused.* She has been *afflicted, tossed with tempest, and not comforted.*

But God! What glory there is in that small but dynamic

thought! In verse 10, it says *for mountains shall depart, and the hills be removed, but my kindness shall not depart from thee.* God is truly the Lover of our souls! He is the Faithful One. When all else around us seems to crumble, He stands firm. Though written to that forsaken woman, we can picture that it is written, in essence, to all women. We are God's workmanship. He knew us before we were brought forth in birth. He formed us in our mother's womb. He made each of us a woman by His eternal decree. In this chapter, let us explore the beauty and wonder of that fact. God, Himself, the Faithful One, the One who loves us beyond all others, made us each who we are!

Many in this modern age do not seem content with "who they are." How very sad. God has a wonderful plan for each life. No matter what the world has thrown at you, He offers to draw you to Himself in love. If your mountains seem to crumble, your friends forsake you, even if you are the woman whose husband has left you, you are still God's beloved. He still has that beautiful place of dwelling with Him each day that shines softly with rich jewels of grace and paths of peace. Come around the corner, dear lady. If you are walking on the forest paths where everything seems dark and obscured, then turn the corner to view the secure place of God's delight. Learn how really wonderful it is to be a woman.

No matter if you are a woman in a loving husband and wife relationship, or a widow with fond memories of a life well lived, or a single woman who has a fullness in her life with the Lord, God has that pleasant path that leads to His special place for you. There is purpose in life and that purpose can be best found when we acknowledge the real honor there is in being a woman of God's design.

Do you see that picture of the place of peace and beauty which is found only as we give ourselves to God? We must give ourselves uniquely, accepting and rejoicing in the fact that He that has made us, made us exactly who we are! Your place of dwelling is full of beauty. You can always return to that place of loveliness found on that path, just off the jumble and darkness of the forest road through the world. You will easily find it as you follow the glow of God's light surrounding your cottage made by His design. It is just a prayer and a commitment away.

There is much to learn about the real joy of womanhood!

Let us journey together on the pathway of pleasant stones.

****

There is one issue that must be met head-on in the study of the Scriptures concerning women. There is the false notion that the God of the Hebrew and Christian Scriptures does not honor women. Some worldly theologians have even said that Jesus and Paul were chauvinists. This is false! It is certainly evident that these persons have not read the Scriptures, or at least have not read them with spiritual understanding. The God of the Bible gives honor and equality to women beyond anything that the ancient or modern world could claim. He is the Maker of all and as such has declared:

There is neither Jew nor Greek, there is neither bond nor free,
there is neither male nor female: for ye are all one in Christ Jesus.
Galatians 3:28

This is not only true in the redeemed of the New Testament in Christ Jesus, but was seen of old. The fact that God held each woman responsible for her actions is evident in His dealings with many of those recorded in the Old Testament. From Eve to Rachel, to Miriam and others, their sins were accounted unto them. Their victories in life were also recognized by God. They were not valueless vassals or servants. They were made by their Creator God with a purpose and with a soul. In many of the religions of old, this teaching was not always true. Women were accounted as less than a man in relationship to God. How we should praise the Lord that we are deemed as living souls, with equal responsibilities to God as has a man, and also equal opportunities in His kingdom.

There is an encounter during the beginning of applying the Law among the people of Israel. Moses and the leaders were numbering the people and preparing for the crossing over into

Canaan when land would be given to each tribe and each family in that tribe. Most often, we think of the men of leadership in the tribes, the men as heads of families, and it might seem that the women were in the background. But not so. Five daughters of a man named Zelophehad, of the tribe of Manasseh, came to Moses with a matter of great importance. Their father had died in the wilderness wanderings without a male heir. We can guess that some might have thought to take away his inheritance in the new land. But the daughters came with a reasonable request for the matter to be considered, not just for themselves but for any other women in Israel. They said, *Why should the name of our father be done away from among his family, because he hath no son? Give unto us therefore a possession among the brethren of our father. Numbers 27:4* Perhaps others had thought only in terms of men, but the daughters were bringing a right question. In essence, they were saying that as women they had equal rights in the nation. This was so important an issue that Moses took the question directly to the LORD. *And Moses brought their cause before the LORD. Numbers 27:5* He did not demean them or dismiss them. He did not make light of their claim or ask them to be under submission to male relatives. He brought the matter directly to God. We can almost see Moses standing solemnly before these women as the princes and the congregation of Israel surrounded him before the door of the tabernacle. Moses treated the sisters with honor.

The Lord responded saying, *The daughters of Zelophehad speak right: thou shalt surely give them a possession of an inheritance among their father's brethren, and thou shalt cause the inheritance of their father to pass unto them. Numbers 27:7* Not only was this a decision for just these five women, but God went on to declare that it was for all time in Israel. God had declared, and Moses had taken that declaration to the congregation of Israel, that women have rights! There was no revolution necessary, no protests, God had spoken.

How does this account make you feel about the honor given to women in the Bible?

****

And being in Bethany in the house of Simon the leper, as he sat at meat,
there came a woman having an alabaster box of ointment of spikenard very precious;
and she brake the box, and poured it on his head.
Mark 14:3

Once again, it is highlighted in our minds that it was *a woman* who entered the place of feasting and gave honor to Jesus that day. The Scripture does not say "a person," but specifically, "a woman." God wants us to know exactly what took place! He wants us to honor that woman's testimony. If it had been in another culture of that day, a woman might have been stopped at the doorway. Or she might have been taken away from the guest's presence before she could perform her act. While it took bravery and a steadfastness of purpose to enter with the alabaster box, in Mary there must have been a special confidence as a woman. God had already given examples in His Holy Word of the women of Israel who were deemed as equal vessels, not vassals! There must also have been a calmness of heart because Mary knew Jesus. He was that Perfect One. He would react in the Perfect Way. Mary knew Jesus and Jesus knew Mary. He knew what courage it took for her of gentle soul to walk into that feast. He knew her devotion, He had seen her sit at His feet as He taught. But more importantly, Jesus knew her woman's heart. He knew why she was breaking the alabaster box and why she was anointing Him. Jesus honored her as a woman and as an example of devotion and knowledge of Him for all to see, male or female.

Throughout the Scripture, God honored different women for

their unique part in His plan. Some of those examples are in the Old Testament. They were in scrolls Mary would have been taught. She was well acquainted with the honor and joy it was to be a woman.

Miriam: sister of Moses.   Used of God in the position of a girl and a woman during the deliverance of Israel from Egypt.

Read Exodus 2:1-10. Tell of Miriam's special actions as a maiden of bravery:

Read Exodus 15:20. Tell of Miriam's unique example to the women of Israel:

Read Micah 6:4 and tell of how God wanted the Israelites to remember Miriam:

Deborah: judge of Israel.   Used of God to encourage the men of Israel to be brave and faithful.

Read Judges 4:1-5. Does there seem to be any surprise that a woman was judging Israel?

Read Judges 4:6-7. How important is it that Deborah listened to God?

Read Judges 4:8-9.   Even though Barak seems to be a mighty man of battle, he is fearful to go against the enemies of Israel. Why do you think he asked Deborah to go with him?

Read Judges 4:14. Who did Deborah acknowledge as the

Leader of Israel's troops?

Judges Chapter Five is the Song of Deborah and there is a richness and fullness in the entire chapter! At the end of the song, Deborah gives a glorious summary to those that follow the Lord. Read Judges 5:31 and comment on what you learn about Deborah's primary message to Israel:

Ruth: The Moabite woman who forsakes all for God.   An example of total faithfulness in the time of the Judges when there often was lack of faithfulness throughout Israel.
Read Ruth 1:11-18.
What did you note about Ruth's commitment to Naomi, her mother-in-law?

What did you note about Ruth's commitment to the One true God?

Why do you think Ruth called God "LORD?"

Read Ruth 2:8-12.
How did God provide protection for Ruth that would be important to a young woman?

What tells you in verse ten that Ruth was a humble person?

Read verse twelve out loud. There is a singular beauty in that verse. What two things did God reward Ruth for?

How important was it for others to know that Ruth trusted in God?

Read Ruth 3:9-11.
How could others know that Ruth was a virtuous woman?

Knowing that she is going to be the grandmother of King David, how important do you think it is that she was placed into a godly relationship with a man (Boaz)?

Priscilla: New Testament Jewish Christian who aided Paul
Mightily used of God
Read Acts 18:1-3. From this short passage, how can you know:
That Priscilla and her husband were faithful in their religious identity while in Rome?

That Priscilla and her husband were diligent in their work?

That Priscilla and her husband were taught of Paul?

Read Acts 18:24-28.
Comment on how God used Priscilla and Aquilla to be faithful witnesses of the truth of the Gospel to Apollos:

Knowing that Apollos became a mighty preacher of the Gospel and co-laborer of Paul the Apostle, how does this encourage you in realizing the importance of your witness to others?

Read Romans 16:3-5a.
How committed were Priscilla and Aquila to the cause of the Gospel?

What are your thoughts on the faithfulness of Priscilla to her husband?

Mary, mother of Jesus: Especially chosen of God
Faithful, Blessed
Read Luke 1:26-28.
Break down what the angel said to Mary in phrases and tell what each means to you in your understanding of Mary:
Hail, thou art highly favoured:

The Lord is with thee:

Blessed art thou among women:

Read Luke 1:38:
How does this speak to your heart about being totally committed and totally trusting in God?

How blessed is it to know that Mary, a woman, was chosen to care for the Son of God on earth?

Read Luke 1:46-55. (this is often called The Magnificat or Mary's Song of Praise)

What did you learn the most from reading this passage?

Who did Mary give praise to?

What does Mary call God in verse 47?

How significant is this in your understanding of Mary?

Read John 19:25.
Many of the disciples hid during the crucifixion, but standing at the foot of the Cross is Mary and other women. How does this impress you about loyalty, bravery and total commitment?

Read Acts 1:12-14: following Jesus' Ascension into Heaven.
Does it surprise you to see Mary amongst the believers gathered together in Jerusalem?

Read Acts 2:1-5: The Day of Pentecost

Have you considered that Mary was probably in the group that received the Holy Spirit that day? What an honor! How exciting it must have been to Mary, who may have been often criticized by others, to see this mighty demonstration of God's power!

Why do you think that Mary remained faithful to the message of the Gospel, no matter what others said?

Look back to Mary's answer to the Angel Gabriel, in the Annunciation. (Luke 1:38) We could count that as her moment of total giving of herself to God. How important is it for you as a woman to know a specific time that you gave your heart to God in total faith, believing His Word?

How would you like to be "blessed of God?"

****

It is significant in looking at these women who are praised in their womanhood, to remember Ruth. Her fellow sister-in-law, Orpha, had the same opportunity to follow Naomi to Israel, but there was one huge difference. Only Ruth had given herself as a woman totally to God. Naomi had said that there was no possibility of her having any more sons to offer to her daughters-in-law. There was also the possibility that in the land of Israel, a foreigner of Moab would not be viewed as marriage potential. To go with Naomi, to accept her God, Ruth had to give up all hope of a future of marriage. She had to lay on the altar of commitment the one thing that seemed to be the most honorable for a woman of her day, to be a wife. Any thought of little children calling her mother, had to be removed. What she gave up was a total life dream for many. Orpha turned back. She doubtless found a new husband among the Moabites. Her destiny and future are lost to us in time. But Ruth, who gave all of womanhood to God, is remembered to this day. She seems to walk in grace through the fields of Bethlehem with her godly husband Boaz at her side, and their little children laughing in play. Ruth made the choice of greatest value. She gave of herself as a woman to God, and God fulfilled all dreams and destiny as a woman beyond all that she could have thought to ask for in life. She had truly come to rest under the wings of the LORD God of Israel. There was the place of peace. There was the place of care. There was the place of fulfillment.

****

There are many unique characteristics that are noted to be valued in women as discussed in the Bible. We will touch on just a few here. There are so many more! When we study these characteristics, we can more deeply realize what a unique privilege it is to be a woman chosen and redeemed by God. There are things that are unique and blessed just for us, others that either men or women can enjoy. When we are comfortable with being who we are made to be, there are no struggles, no bitterness, no competition within ourselves or with others. When we think of ourselves as individuals made by God, there is peace and purpose. What a glory and blessing it is to be a woman! Again, let us study a few womanly characteristics:

A gracious, devotional spirit:
> I Peter 3:1-2, Proverbs 11:16

Gifted by God:
> Exodus 35:25-26, Proverbs 31:13

Ministry to others:
> Proverbs 31:20, Matthew 27:55, Romans 16:1-2, 12

Unique value of virtue:
> Proverbs 11:16, 12:4, 31:10, 30

There are so many other godly characteristics that seem magnified in a woman. But there are also the unique privileges and relationships of a woman. It is simplistic, but only women get to be mothers! Only women get the joy of feeling that first flutter of movement of the baby within. Only women get the peaceful blessing of nursing a baby. Only women can always know that the child, then adult, once dwelt beneath her heart. In marriage, the blessing of being loved by one man is marvelous to a woman's soul. God knows our needs, and part of that is to be a partner. If a woman is single, then her relationship with others and with her God will often be increased in the supply of her own needs. These relationships are beautified by a woman's touch.

There are times when Jesus speaks with women in the Gospels, that we can hear a tenderness in His voice, an honor in His way of addressing them.

Read the following verses. Comment on the special interaction of Jesus with the woman involved:

Matthew 9:20-22

Matthew 15:22-28

Matthew 28:5-10

Mark 3:34-35

Mark 12:41-44

Luke 10:38-42

Luke 13:10-17

John 4:4-30, 39-42

John 8:3-11

John 11:1-33

John 12:1-8

John 20:11-18

The vivid descriptions of Jesus in the Gospels, allow us to enter into each scene. Being there, we can often hear the tenderness in His voice. Each of the women heard it, too, and knew He was the Lord that understood their needs. He was courteous to each one and honoring of their personhood.

Tell what you think Jesus' assessment of the value of a woman is?

****

Jesus made the comment in Luke 13:34: *O Jerusalem, Jerusalem, which killest the prophets, and stonest them that are sent unto thee; how often would I have gathered thy children together, as a hen doth gather her brood under her wings, and ye would not!* One can almost hear the groan in His voice. There is a sadness, but also compassionate love in that statement. The city of Jerusalem held a special place in Israel's history. It was also the place God had chosen for the temple to be built and rebuilt. Yet, in that city that should have been filled with holiness, there were those that rejected God's prophets and subverted God's laws. It was in that city that Jesus would be tried and sent to the Cross. As God the Son, Jesus knew all these things, yet He still had love. In describing His love for the city and its inhabitants, He used the example of a mother's love: a hen who protects her chicks against all danger. As women, most of us can understand that type of gathering love. There is a tremendous value that Jesus gives to the heart issues of a woman. Yes, men can know deep emotions and have commitments unique and powerful to them. What is studied here is not to diminish that which is of excellent value for men to serve as examples to us all. The duties, responsibilities and leadership of men, does not diminish the unique value there is in being a woman.

God had a reason that He created both male and female. In Creation, God declared it good! *And God saw every thing that he had made, and, behold, it was very good... Genesis 1:31* Using Hebrew meanings of the words *very* and *good,* we could understand it as: exceedingly best, precious and rich in value. The Creation of both male and female was exceedingly more wonderful than we could ever imagine! That should make each of us as women be filled with wonder and awe toward our Creator. We should rejoice in the fact that we are women, and realize, once again, the great privilege that is ours to live out our lives in God's perfect purpose planned uniquely for each of us. There are mighty and powerful things a woman can do in that living. There is a liberty in the freedom of being a redeemed daughter of the Great God. We need to embrace it and live it out for others to see.

What do you see as the greatest blessings there are in your personal life gained through totally giving of your womanhood to God?

Write a personal prayer of commitment of yourself as a woman to God:

****

So God created man in his own image,
in the image of God created he him; male and female created he
them.
Genesis 1:27

****

Mary folded the garment she had worn to Simon's house.
She put it carefully into the chest in her room.
Her hands softly touched the special items within.
Some her mother had passed down to her.
Some she had sewn with dreams in each stitch.
There was the marriage veil her grandmother had worn.
Carefully wrapped in a linen cloth.
It had carried the dreams of others.
Dreams of womanhood,
Dreams of candle light and music,
Dreams of commitment and love.
Mary wondered if those dreams would ever come into her life?
Would her eyes look through the openings in the veil,
Woven on the lace maker's loom?

Would there be a marriage for her one day?
A soft breeze came in through the window of her room,
The light from her candle standing near the chest flickered.
Mary paused and sank to her knees.

All of who Mary was she laid out to God that night.
The dreams of the veil,
The wonderings of her heart,
The essence of who she was as a woman.
Mary knew then the meaning of total commitment of self.

She whispered into the candle lit room:
Lord, my God,
Your way is best for me.
Whether I ever wear the marriage veil,
Or just save it for another,
It is good in my soul.
Whether I carry a child within,
Or just wipe a little one's brow,
in the village square.
It is good in my soul.
Whether I am known for my ministries,
Or just aid with the work of others,
It is good in my soul.
Lord, my God,
Thank You for making me a woman.
I can see the wisdom of that plan,
I accept the duties and honor it holds.
Help me to serve You with all I am,
As a person uniquely made for Your service.
Help me to encourage others,
As a person especially made for each moment
Of service for You.

Help me to be the woman You want me to be;
From this moment on.

Mary, stayed on her knees for a few moments in adoring love,
Wrapped in the time she had spent with her Creator God.
Then she arose.
Once more she smoothed the veil,
Then closed the lid to the wooden chest.
It was good with her soul.

Chapter Twelve
Tokens of Remembrance

Part of the treasure given to us as Christians are tokens of remembrance to be kept close to our hearts and lived in our lives. They remind us of the unspeakable, tremendous, indescribable gift of Christ. The prayer of our hearts and the wonder of our praise should always be based on the truth of II Corinthians 9:15: *Thanks be unto God for his unspeakable gift.* Words cannot fully express the gratitude we should have to God. The word *unspeakable* in Greek, means just that: indescribable. Nothing in all of history, nothing in modern society, and certainly nothing in other "religions," can surpass the gift of Christ given to us to secure our salvation. Nothing can outshine, out-value, out-live that gift given by God. Oh, what great love. To help us in our remembrance of this great love and gift, God has given us tokens of remembrance. Just as the children of Israel were to sit together at the remembrance of the Passover to observe certain significant reminders of that event, so these tokens of remembrance are to remind us of God's grace. Some are observances and some are heart felt reminders, but all point to Christ, our unspeakable gift received in salvation.

Mark 14:3-9
And being in Bethany in the house of Simon the leper, as he sat at meat,
there came a woman having an alabaster box of ointment of spikenard very precious;
and she brake the box, and poured it on his head.
And there were some that had indignation within themselves, and said,
Why was this waste of the ointment made?

For it might have been sold for more than three hundred pence, and have been given to the poor. And they murmured against her.
And Jesus said, Let her alone; why trouble ye her? She hath wrought a good work on me.
For ye have the poor with you always, and whensoever ye will ye may do them good:
but me ye have not always.
She hath done what she could:
she is come aforehand to anoint my body to the burying.
Verily I say unto you,
Wheresoever this gospel shall be preached throughout the whole world,
this also that she hath done shall be spoken of for a memorial of her.

When Mary entered the place of feasting that day, she was doing so in order to honor a remembrance of what she had heard Jesus say at an earlier time. He had said that He would die in Jerusalem. Mary understood what Jesus had said, and she remembered His words. It seemed that something in His preaching and teaching laid the eminence of His death upon her heart. She felt certain that there might not be a future time when she could tell Him she understood. There might not be another time when she personally could anoint Him with the oil for burial. There might not be a better time to show Jesus the honor and devotion that was His in her thoughts. There might not be that "other" time, but the occasion of the feast gave a present time for her to do this singular act of love for Jesus. He would understand, and that Mary knew of a certainty.

Perhaps every time Mary looked at the alabaster box in her bedchamber and smelled the faint hint of its contents through the invisible cracks of its ancient seal, she had thought, "He is going to die, die for me." She knew that she wanted to pour out that ointment on Jesus in gratitude for what He would do. Her concern must have been whether she would be allowed to do it after His certain death. She did not know exactly when that would happen, but she trusted

His words and knew that it would come to pass. "Do it ahead of time," must have come the whisper of her soul, or was it of the Holy Spirit, Himself, we do not know. But we do know that she did it as a token of her belief and faith in the coming sacrifice. Jesus said what she did that day would be a remembrance of her for all time. But it was also a remembrance from Mary's heart of what He would do that would last for all time. He died that we might live!

Mary's sister Martha had answered Jesus' question in understanding of His Person and work in John 11:25-27. *Jesus said unto her, I am the resurrection, and the life: he that believeth in me, though he were dead, yet shall he live: And whosoever liveth and believeth in me shall never die. Believest thou this? She saith unto him, Yea, Lord: I believe that thou art the Christ, the Son of God, which should come into the world.* After her answer, which I have always treasured as being one of the strongest declarations of belief in Jesus in the New Testament, Martha went to call Mary secretly from the house. Her call was simply, *The Master is come, and calleth for thee. John 11:28.* It seems both sisters had strong faith and had, perhaps, discussed many times all the things they believed about Jesus and what He taught. What a blessed privilege was theirs. But it is our privilege, also, as we can read these words in our Bibles and believe the truths about Jesus for ourselves. We, too, must rise up and come to honor Him. What Jesus did for us should be in our remembrance for <u>all times</u>, not just for a time, but all times.

I wonder if after the feast was done and all the men had gone out, whether Martha and Mary came into the place of feasting to help clean up. They would have certainly been the ones to treasure the broken pieces of the Alabaster Box laying there. They would have seen the remnants of the oil on the floor and smelled of its fragrance. I wonder, did they gently pick up each piece of the box and wrap it in fine linen. Perhaps some of the oil was wiped up with another cloth. Did Mary take those things to her room afterwards? Did future visitors to the home in Bethany scent the fragrance wafting through the doorway? Was it then that the sisters could witness that, indeed, Jesus was the Resurrection and the Life? They could testify that He had died but rose again! What a cherished thought. Two sisters, personalities woven together for service to their Lord.

I wonder, does our life testify of Jesus? Does the fragrance of our deeds and our words reach out to bring pleasure to others and witness of Him? Oh, to have just one ounce of the ointment of remembrance in our possession would be a marvelous thing! Yet we do have remembrances and testimonies that speak to our minds and can be shared with others. They should be as meaningful as a tangible piece of alabaster or a scent of ointment most rare. They are the tokens of remembrance that God has so graciously gifted to us, because of His great love.

What are some of the tokens of remembrance that God has given to us to cherish? We will study some of them in this chapter:

1) **The Lord's Supper**:

In Matthew 26:2, Jesus once again told the disciples of His coming death. He declared: *Ye know that after two days is the feast of the Passover, and the Son of man is betrayed to be crucified.* The date was even given clearly, but nothing seems to be said by any. Calmly, steadily Jesus was making His way to the Cross. But first there would be that treasured time that we often call The Last Supper. On the day of the Passover, some of the disciples were sent ahead to prepare the meal, a token of remembrance for the Jews, in a borrowed upper room. *Now when the even was yet come, he sat down with the twelve. Matthew 26:20.* As soon as Jesus was alone with the disciples, he spoke of the meaning of the token of remembrance He is giving to them, to be remembered after His death: *And as they were eating, Jesus took bread, and blessed it, and brake it, and gave it to the disciples, and said, Take, eat; this is my body. And he took the cup, and gave thanks, and gave it to them saying, Drink ye all of it; For this is my blood of the new testament, which is shed for many for the remission of sins. Matthew 26:26-28.* This is recorded again in Mark 14:22-24. In Luke 22:14-20, the application of remembrance is strengthened: *And when the hour was come, he sat down, and the twelve apostles with him. And he said unto them, With desire I have desired to eat this Passover with you before I suffer: For I say unto you, I will not any more eat thereof, until it be fulfilled in the kingdom of God. And he took the cup, and gave thanks, and said, Take this, and divide it among yourselves: For I say unto you, I will not drink of the fruit of the vine, until the kingdom of God shall come. And he took bread, and gave thanks, and brake it, and gave unto them, saying, This is my body which is given for you: this do in remembrance of me. Likewise also the cup after supper, saying This cup is the new testament in my blood, which is shed for you.* The Apostle Paul explains this token of remembrance to all that would read the Epistle of I Corinthians. Paul did not want the saved ones to forget the immensity of meaning in that practice that we call The Lord's Supper. It had become an activity of the New Testament church already, just years after Jesus' death, burial and resurrection. To some in the Corinthian church, it had become a time of gathering, of feasting, but not of remembrance of the great sacrifice of Christ. So Paul clearly reminds them, and us, of the true meaning of this time of remembrance: *For I have received of the Lord that which also I delivered unto you, That the Lord Jesus the same night in which he was betrayed took bread: And when he had given thanks, he brake it, and said, Take, eat, this is my body, which is broken for you: this do in remembrance of me. After the same manner also he took the cup, when he had supped, saying, This cup is the new testament in my blood: this do ye, as oft as ye drink it, in remembrance of me. For as often as ye eat this bread, and drink this cup, ye do shew the Lord's death till he come. I Corinthians 11:23-26.*

Read I Corinthians 11:23-26 again. Listen in your mind to the tenderness of Paul's voice as he reveals the depth of meaning and the token of remembrance of The Lord's Supper. What high lights do you get from this re-reading?

How significant is it to know that the actual Last Supper was before Jesus' death on the Cross?

Read I Corinthians 11:27-30. Comment on the seriousness of self-examination by believers before they partake of the Lord's Supper.

It is worthy of note that The Lord's Supper is not a payment for sin. Only the shed blood and death of Jesus Christ on the Cross of Calvary was that payment. It is a remembrance of the redemption which was won on the Cross. Sadly, through the ages, some have thought The Lord's Supper more than a token of remembrance, but a sacrifice to be observed over and over again, as if Jesus could be put to death over and over again. What tragedy. That is why we need to always treasure the true meaning, a token to our hearts and minds of the true sacrifice, once for all.

Read Hebrews 10:10-14, and comment on how that affects your understanding of the true meaning of The Lord's Supper:

Often as we gather together to partake of The Lord's Supper, the words of I Corinthians 11 are read by the pastor. During that time of reflection, I often gaze at the small cup I have been given to hold while we are praying. The sanctuary lights reflect in the redness of the juice held within that little cup, and I pause to remember. I remember Jesus, Blessed Jesus, hanging on that Cross for me personally. It is a very blessed, quiet time of remembrance and gratitude. How blessed we are that the Lord knew our hearts so well that He gave us this remembrance, lest we forget.

2) **The Ordinance of Baptism**:

In almost every church covenant, there is a section called: The Ordinances. In that classification will be two tokens of remembrance: The Lord's Supper and Baptism. Notice that these are not defined as "Rituals," but as Ordinances. Ordinances are those things that were commanded by the Bible to be performed within the local church. A command from Scripture is solemn indeed. By contrast, a Ritual is an observance that is following the dictates of man. Perhaps you even have personal rituals in your own life. There is the simple ritual of brushing your teeth upon awakening in the morning and again before going to bed at night. Many people have a night time ritual of checking all the doors leading to the outside of their home to make sure that they are secured and locked. While these rituals are important in our lives, they are not ordained by God. Likewise, in many religious organizations, rituals perform an immense time slot of what they observe. People can become enchanted with rituals. That is one of the direct consequences of control within a church system. Even that which is ordained of God will often become entrenched in the system of ritual. The Lord's Supper will become that which is abundant in ritual and exact replication each time it occurs. Baptism will become part of a prescribed ritual. We must break through that which is ritual, that which is misunderstood, and that which is contrary to the Word of God, in order to find that which is true and beautiful in meaning as a token of remembrance.

Having been a missionary in an area that had the entrenchment of ritual within its religious heritage, I can attest to the joy and sense of liberty for new believers that the realization of the truth of the Biblical meaning of The Lord's Supper and of Baptism really was to have in their lives. It was like they were set free from the constraint of rituals, to walk in the truth of the liberty they now had in Christ. That liberty was intricately woven with the knowledge of the truth of the Gospel. Both Ordinances of a church are to be Tokens of Remembrance of the Death, Burial and Resurrection of Christ.

There is a holy commitment that surrounds Baptism. It is indeed the public declaration of that which a person has believed in their lives. It is a new believer taking a stand for that which is true and liberating, that which is life changing and life affirming. Baptism is a sacred remembrance indeed. It is a vivid picture of the Death, Burial, and Resurrection of Christ which one has believed in at the time of salvation. It is not salvation itself, but a mighty and glorious declaration of the validity of salvation graced through faith.

It is interesting then that there should be controversy concerning this solemn but joyous ordinance. To answer those questions, let us study some Biblical references to Baptism:

The Preparation for Messiah, the Preaching and Baptism of John the Baptist:
Read Matthew 3:4-6,11, Mark 1:3-4, Luke 3:16.

Explain what John the Baptist's "job" was:

Tell what you think the baptism of John meant according to these verses:

Think and comment on this statement: "The baptism of John was to show forth a belief in repentance, the recognition of sin, and the near coming of the Messiah."

Read Luke 7:26-30: "Those that believed John's preaching were baptized and those that rejected the counsel of God were ____ baptized of him!"

What did it mean to reject the counsel of God?

The Baptism of Jesus:
Read Matthew 3:13-17.
Why did Jesus say he came to be baptized of John?

Did Jesus ever say that He needed to be baptized for remission of sins?

Why do you think John at first did not want to baptize Jesus?

Tell how you think the voice from Heaven encouraged John:

How does what happened that day affect you?

The True meaning of Christian baptism:
Read Acts 10:36-43, 11:16-18.
Peter is preaching concerning the truth of God. What do you find significant in these verses referring to baptism?

Read Acts 8:26-38.
What did the eunuch believe in?

What did Philip say was necessary for the eunuch before he could be baptized?

How do you know that the baptism was by immersion? (Read verses 38-39)

Read Acts 2:21:
What must a person do to be saved?

Read Acts 2:38:
The Greek word used in the verse that is translated "for" has the meaning of "as a result of." We use that English word "for" in many ways, one of which is the meaning of the Greek here. How does that enhance your understanding of the definition of baptism's meaning?

Now Read Acts 2:41. What had the people done before they were baptized?

Read Romans 6:4-5.
Equate Scriptural baptism with a remembrance of what Christ did for us:

What is the commitment that we are to make following our baptism?

Read Colossians 2:6-7, 12.
Comment on these verses:

Comment on how this Scriptural study on baptism has helped you to understand its true meaning:

To be the Token of Remembrance and the Ordinance that God intended, baptism must: represent the Death, Burial and Resurrection of Jesus Christ, and be a testimony of what we have believed by faith that resulted in our salvation.

3) <u>**Remembrances through special days of the church year**</u>.
Even though we are not to be given to rituals, there are those special holidays that we celebrate throughout the year, year by year, that serve as Tokens of Remembrance. These are especially meaningful when we consider the strength that we are to help build in our children and "children's children" in celebrating Christ in their lives.

God does not want us to be "entangled' with earthly rituals and observances. This can extend to the many days which are known as "holy days" in ritualistic churches. While there is a wealth of value in remembering the Tokens of Remembrances given to us as Christians in relation to Christ, there is a danger in expanding those days to include celebrations of those a church has labeled as "Saints," also those days added to be kept as rituals. This warning is given in the Book of Galatians.

Read Galatians 4:9-11, 5:1. Explain the burden that Paul had for those in Galatia who were bound by observances:

How can that relate to our liberty in Christ?

Why would the obsession with observing the days and months and times and years dictated by a religious organization turn our minds away from true faith?

Note how a proper "celebration" of the holidays of Easter (Resurrection Sunday) and Christmas can be used to encourage growth in our family unity and faith:

Moses warned the people of Israel of the necessity to help their children remember the importance of the statues of God once they entered into the land of Canaan. Read Deuteronomy 6:1-13. Explain why this was so important to the families of the Israelites:

How can we translate this concept into our modern Christian lives?

Relate some ways that the celebrations of Easter and Christmas have blessed and built up your life of faith:

We are to rejoice in the "law of liberty" and not be bound by restrictions of the law.

Comment on why you think some cults forbid the observances of Christian holidays?

Comment on why some formalized religions (even outside of Christianity) stress holy days and observances?

Write a prayer of thankfulness to God for the true gift of faith given by grace, which is not dependent on our observances of rituals:

Having come out of a system of worship that involved many rituals and special days, I can personally testify to the beauty I found in the true observance of the special holidays of remembrance of Christ in my life. Easter (Resurrection Day) found its true meaning and gave an eternal depth of gratitude to the Lord for the victory of the Risen Christ. Christmas became a season of joy in entering into the wonder of Christ coming to earth for us. No matter if we know not the actual dates of the Nativity, the wonder is still there. To share that with our children and make it a part of their lives, is to strengthen their commitment to that which is real in our Christian lives.

4) **Remembrances of our need of Him**.

Perhaps the most blessed and unique distinction of Biblical Christianity is the promise of the indwelling of the Holy Spirit given unto each of God's born-again children. It is amazing to consider the fulfillment of the promise of Jesus to each of us as complete.

And I will pray the Father, and he shall give you another Comforter,
that he may abide with you for ever.
Even the Spirit of truth; whom the world cannot receive,
because it seeth him not, neither knoweth him:
but ye know him; for he dwelleth with you, and shall be in you...
John 14:16-17

But the Comforter, which is the Holy Ghost, whom the Father will send in my name,
he shall teach you all things, and bring all things to your remembrance,
whatsoever I have said unto you.
John 14:26

God knows our every need. One of the most pressing needs we have is to be in constant communication with our God. Above and beyond all that we could ever imagine in our own effort to sustain this with our prayers and devotions, is the constant present abiding of the Holy Spirit within. He is not a guest that we are to entertain, but the reality of God to instruct, comfort, and sustain us day by day. He is not a visitor that could depart for a far land, but a permanent resident in our lives. Oh, Glory beyond all words to explain! The Holy Spirit is the One who is there to bring to our attention the Tokens of Remembrance we are to have in our Christian lives. He is the One who gently reminds us of our needs. When we think to try to do things in our own strength, we will feel that reminder of our need of God's strength.

Read II Corinthians 3:4-5. Comment on what you think the phrase "our sufficiency is of God" means in relation to our needs in life:

Correlate the need for prayer in relationship to Ephesians 3:16 becoming a place of victory in your life:

Why do we need to be "strengthened with might by his Spirit in the inner man"?

With reverence of heart, read Isaiah 40: 28-31 and comment on how this reminds you of your great need for the Lord's strength:

Read Isaiah 41:10. Reflect on how the promise of this verse encourages you:

The indwelling of the Holy Spirit brings to our minds constant remembrances of God in each step of our Christian walk. The Tokens of Remembrances He gives to us are as pillars placed along the path of life. They are as altars of worship we need to stop at throughout the day. They are precious stones piled one on another that remind us that our God is real.

5) **Remembrance of our need to give our honor, commitment, and acknowledgment of who God is, what He did, does, and will do**.

Wherefore David blessed the LORD before all the congregation: and David said,
Blessed be thou, LORD God of Israel our father, for ever and ever.
Thine, O LORD, is the greatness, and the power, and the glory, and the victory, and the majesty:
For all that is in the heaven and in the earth is thine;
Thine is the kingdom, O LORD, and thou art exalted as head above all things.
Both riches and honour come of thee, and thou reignest over all;
And in thy hand is power and might;
and in thy hand is to make great, and to give strength unto all.
Now therefore, our God, we thank thee, and praise thy glorious name.

...

Keep this for ever in the imagination of the thoughts of the heart of
thy people,
and prepare their heart unto thee…
I Chronicles 29:10-13, 18

One of the greatest Tokens of Remembrance in our lives is to simply remember God! I love the phrase, "God awareness."

Oh Lord,
Make me ever aware of You,
Each breath that I take,
Each step that I make,
Let me be aware of Your presence with me.
Help me to open my eyes to the wonders around me,
And remember that You are the Creator of all.
Help me to open my heart to those You send my way,
And remember that You molded each life.
Help me to open my mind to the lessons from Your Word,
And remember that You wrote each line.
Help me to be aware of You.

Write a prayer for honor and praise to the Lord:

6) **Remembrances for prayer**

Prayer is a vital part of the Christian life. In fact, it is one of the unique realities that set Christians apart from other religions. While those that worship idols may seem to offer prayer and make offerings, the reality is that idols are man-made objects or things of nature that cannot answer what they cannot hear.

…the work of men's hands, wood and stone,
which neither see, nor hear, nor eat nor smell.
Deuteronomy 4:28
Their idols are silver and gold, the work of men's hands.

They have mouths, but they speak not: eyes have they, but they see not.
Psalm 115:4-5
... they have no knowledge that set up the wood of their graven image,
and pray unto a god that cannot save.
Isaiah 45:20

Prayer is communication. God hears our prayers and He is always there for us. The cry of the human heart is found in Job 31:35: *Oh, that one would hear me! Behold, my desire is, that the Almighty would answer me...* The cry of victory for the Christian is that there is One that hears us! It is our God.

Hear me when I call, O God of my righteousness...
The LORD will hear when I call unto him.
Psalm 4:1,3
In my distress I called upon the LORD, and cried unto my God:
He heard my voice out of his temple, and my cry came before him,
even into his ears.
Psalm 18:6
The righteous cry, and the LORD heareth...
Psalm 34:17
The LORD ... heareth the prayer of the righteous.
Proverbs 15:29
Therefore I will look unto the LORD;
I will wait for the God of my salvation: my God will hear me.
Micah 7:7

We do not have to cry in the desperation of no hope. Our God is our Hope. *Oh, that one would hear me* is already answered. It is answered in the surety of the reality of God. That same God reminds us when we need to pray. It is a Token of Remembrance that He will not let us go without that sweet communion of prayer. It is manna to our souls and a balm unto our hearts to talk to our God. We do not have to be experiencing a trial or danger to cry out to Him, He is also there to hear our whispered prayers of devotion and praise. Our strength comes on wings of eagles as we turn our hearts in prayer to God.

Jesus gave us His reminder of our need to pray in Luke 18:1: *And he spake unto them to this end, that men ought always to pray, and not to faint.* He wants us to be strong in His might, to stand true and to always know that He is a personal God. Prayer is our communion with Him. Often, the Holy Spirit will remind of our need to pray by giving us a burden in our hearts. There are even times that I have been awakened in the middle of the night and know beyond a shadow of a doubt that God is calling on me to pray. I may not know what or who I am praying for, but God knows and it is enough. It is a solid pillar of remembrance that God shares that burden with our hearts.

Likewise the Spirit also helpeth our infirmities:
for we know not what we should pray for as we ought:
but the Spirit itself maketh intercession for us with groanings which
cannot be uttered.
And he that searcheth the hearts knoweth what is the mind of the
Spirit,
because he maketh intercession for the saints according to the will of
God.
Romans 8:26-27

What a wonderful, loving God we have. He is high and lifted up, yet He desires to communicate with us. When we cannot fully know how to pray, He prays for us. Glory. This one fact so impacted my life at a time of extreme illness, when I could not even seem to put my thoughts together in prayer. Yet, God knew! The touch of the moment when I remembered the verses in Romans Eight have continued throughout my life to be the solid assurance found in the song: "My God is real, real in my soul!" Prayer is indeed a Token of

Remembrance of the reality of God and the truth of our fellowship with Him. Never doubt, dear Christian, your God is real!

7) **Remembrances to take a stand for God**.

Many Christians live in a comfortable world. While there may be some criticism of their religious beliefs and standards, the comfortable world does not include life threatening persecution. That has not always been so. Throughout the ages, there have been multitudes of believers who became martyrs of the faith, because they would not back down from a faithful stand for the Lord Jesus and for God's Word. Even today, in parts of the world, to take a stand for Christ is to put your physical life in jeopardy. We need to take a sobering look at the truth of what it means to take a stand for Christ. When we think of those for whom such a stand might mean death, we are humbled to even consider the many times we may have failed to take a stand for our faith, or made it a quiet commitment. "Stand up, stand up for Jesus," are not just the uplifting words of a standard church hymn, they are commands that should ring true in our hearts. If we stand for Jesus, we are holding the banner high that says, "I am a Christian."

Jesus warned that standing for Him would not always be the easy way:

Blessed are ye, when men shall revile you, and persecute you,
and shall say all manner of evil against you falsely, for my sake.
Matthew 5:11
And ye shall be hated of all men for my name's sake… Matthew
10:22

Likewise, we are reminded again in the New Testament of what taking a stand for Jesus can mean:

And they departed from the presence of the council,
rejoicing that they were counted worthy to suffer shame for his name.
Acts 5:41

Choosing rather to suffer affliction with the people of God,
Than to enjoy the pleasures of sin for a season. Hebrew 11:15
But the God of all grace, who hath called us unto his eternal glory by
Christ Jesus,
After that ye have suffered a while,
Make you perfect, stablish, strengthen, settle you. I Peter 5:10

Living for Christ takes commitment and courage. In the verses cited above, there is an element of absolute truthful transparency. We are not to suffer for false professions, but choose to be totally committed to that which we have claimed in our hearts. Jesus did not go to the Cross secretly, it was done in the open before many witnesses. If we ever note ourselves faltering in our stand, remember Jesus, remember Him!

Looking unto Jesus the author and finisher of our faith;
Who for the joy that was set before him endured the cross, despising
the shame,
and is set down at the right hand of the throne of God.
For consider him that endured such contradiction of sinners against
himself,
lest ye be wearied and faint in your minds.
Hebrews 12:2-3

8) <u>Remembrance of His promises</u>

There is one statement about God's promises that we must always remember. It is simple, it is direct and it is a Token of Remembrance of Who our God is! Because of God's sterling, immutable character we can know beyond a shadow of a doubt that "All the promises of God to believers are true." Rest in that statement. Stand on the foundation that is sure. Be lifted up in faith and believing, "All the promises of God to believers are true." We could stop right there, but there is a further, strengthening joy in delving into Scriptural verses on God's promises.

There is a unique connection between remembering God's

promises and living out our Christian lives in victory. *Having therefore these promises, dearly beloved, let us cleanse ourselves from all filthiness of the flesh and spirit, perfecting holiness in the fear of God. II Corinthians 7:1.* Tokens of Remembrance should be those that humble us before our God and make us want to be a cleansed and holy people who walk in reverence with Him. What a sobering and challenging commitment we should make.

In II Corinthians 7:1 is an important word: *these.* Paul is reminding the believers that because we have *these promises* we should live holy committed lives. What are *these promises?* To find out the immediate references, we need to look back to II Corinthians chapter 6.

God's promises that we find as we look back into Chapter 6 of II Corinthians:

<u>Verse 2</u>: *I have heard thee in a time accepted, and in the day of salvation have I succoured thee.* What a promise! God has heard us! We do not pray to an empty sky! There is a God of truth and power who hears each of our prayers! How amazing! In the day of our salvation God promises that He succoured us. The Greek word for *succoured* means to give aid. There is a tenderness in that promise. It is as if God has sealed to our souls His eternal protection. Our salvation is sure, it is succoured by our Lord. He draws us tenderly to His breast and there we can rest in peace.

<u>Verse 16</u>: *... ye are the temple of the living God; as God hath said, I will dwell in them, and walk in them; and I will be their God, and they shall be my people.* God promises that He will dwell in us! Glory! The promise of God's eternal intimate presence with us is secure. God will walk in us! We often think of God walking with us, but the promise is so magnified in this verse: God will walk in us! Oh Lord, I need that promise. You walk in me. Where I go You go! How that should direct my paths today! You never stumble, help me to not stumble! Make Your walk in me strong. God promises to be our God! What a mighty promise that is! Think of the Almighty God

of all Creation promising to be our God! There could be rivers of words flowing from the writings of our daily journals and they could never exhaust the reality of that promise. He has written our names in His Book of Life! We are His and He is ours! In union with this promise is the sure statement that we shall (absolutely, positively shall) be God's people. Christian, have you thought to walk another pathway today, to speak another type of language, to commune with the things of this world? Have you considered your citizenship? You are a person of God. That can never be changed. No matter how far some may try to run, they are a person of God and He will not let them go. He will draw His own with cords of love back into the place they should be. Or else they will be miserable! Do not wander today!

Verse 17: ... *I will receive you.* God calls to His wanderers and says, *Come out... be separate...* When we think to sin, or wander away, we should ever hear the voice of God calling to us, "Come out of that temptation, dear child of Mine. Separate yourself from that which would harm you, be clean not unclean." And then comes the promise: *I will receive you.* How often has a person gone away from communication with their family and decided to come back, but had the thought, "I wonder if they will forgive me and accept me?" With God there is no doubt! He will receive us with the open arms of His love. It is a promise!

Verse 18: *[I] will be a Father unto you, and ye shall be my sons and daughters, saith the Lord Almighty.* There is such a strong need in every human heart to be loved and cared for by our fathers. One of the most moving experiences I have ever witnessed came at the birth of my grandson. It had been a stressful delivery. Standing next to the hospital bed as the doctor lifted the small baby, the father asked in loving concern, "Is he all right?" Immediately that little premature baby turned his head and looked right at his father in response to his voice! The doctor smiled and said. "He will be just fine." In the presence and security of being with our Father, we are just fine, too! There is a strength of bond that ever comforts our hearts and cheers our way. We have a Heavenly Father that has claimed us as His own. When He speaks, we should turn our hearts toward Him and respond. The further promise is entwined with the first, we are God's sons and daughters. There is no disowning, no casting off or denials in God's forever family. He promises us that He has claimed us as His own. He has signed that spiritual birth certificate with the blood of Christ and there is no fading of that document in the files of Heaven! There is a seal on that promise and it is found in the last four words of the verse: *saith the Lord Almighty.* God seals His promise with His own name! God's promises are sure!

There are hundreds of promises in God's Word. Just remember our sentence of the Token of Remembrance in regards to God's promises: "All the promises of God to believers are true."

What promises of God are especially important to you today?

What promise of God do you need to claim today to help give you victory in an area of need?

How has a promise of God challenged you today to confess sin and ask to be made clean?

How do you think you can implement the challenge to perfect holiness in your life?

9) **Remembrance of His Word, lessons learned and challenges to be ever learning.**
Many a patriarch of the Old Testament built up Tokens of Remembrance in places where they had learned a deep lesson from

God. As God deals with us day by day through His Word, we should be challenged to listen and learn, and then build Tokens of Remembrance at that point of decision in our lives. Perhaps, we need to keep a journal of those decisions that we can look back on and remember what commitments we made to our God. Many write a note in the margin of their Bibles to record that spiritual understanding.

Let us take note of the altars of remembrance that some of the Patriarchs built. Read the reference and note what that Patriarch wanted to remember that God had spoken. You may have to look back in the chapter to find the answer.

Genesis 8:20   Noah   God's Words:

Genesis 12:7   Abram   God's Words:

Genesis 26:25   Isaac   God's Words:

Genesis 28:18   Jacob   God's Words:

Exodus 24:4   Moses   God's Words:

Read Joshua 8:30-35. Here Joshua builds an altar to the Lord for praise, thanksgiving, humbleness and remembrance. It is to be a place of commitment for the entire nation of Israel. That commitment was to be predicated on the remembrance of God's words.

Read Joshua 8:35 again. What unique statement do you find there to apply to your life today?

The answer to that question is found in the first phrase of the verse: *There was not a word of all that Moses commanded...* Nothing of God's words to Moses was left out in the reading to the congregation of Israel! Sometimes, it is easy to pick out a verse we want to hear, but we do not consider the ALL of God's Word. There is such an importance for the Christian to be aware of all that the Bible has to say to us. There is to be no shallowness in the Christian life. Just as the Patriarchs of old kept digging wells until water was found, so we are to "dig" into God's Word every day and find there the water of the washing of His Spirit to fill our thirsty souls.

What "altars" of commitment do you need to build today from your personal study of God's Word?

I often call commitment verses "Claiming Verses" for my life. I trust that you will find unique growth in working "Claiming Verses" into your own life journey.

Can you think of a special Claiming Verse from God's Word that you would like to claim today?

10) **Remembrance of the woman with the alabaster box**.

This entire book has been tied to the simple, but profound occurrence of a woman with an alabaster box giving of her devotion to Jesus at a feast in Bethany. The remembrance of that which was done serves as a Token of Remembrance for us. Jesus said, *this also that she hath done shall be spoken of for a memorial of her.* That memorial is for us to treasure in our hearts. There are life lessons to learn from multitudes of persons in the Scripture. God gives us glimpses into the moments of time in real people's lives. Those moments are given for our instruction. Part of learning God's Word is knowing the people He has chosen for us to meet on the pages of Holy Writ. Their character, decisions and relationship to God should have an effect on us.

Write what lesson you learned from the following persons in the Bible and how it could be used in your own life:

Joshua   Joshua 24:14-15

Ruth   Ruth 2:12

Esther   Esther 4:16

Job   Job 19:25

David   Psalm 42:5

Mary   Luke 1:18

Peter   Acts 5:29, 41-42

Finally, write what you find most meaningful in your life from our study of Mark 14:3-9.

God established a memorial for the woman with the Alabaster Box to serve as an honor of remembrance for what she had done unto Jesus. That memorial is not just for Mary, but for each of us to view and to claim for our own lives. It is my prayer that the lessons we have learned together as we have journeyed in this book of study will serve as Tokens of Remembrance to your soul. If you start to falter in courage, walk through that door of commitment with Mary by your side. If you seem distracted by the things of the world, let Jesus fill your entire focus of sight. If the words of others seem to wound you, remember Jesus' commendation that day. If you need to remember what Jesus did for you, enter into the understanding that Mary had gained as she had sat at His feet. If you fear to take a stand for Christ, break open your Alabaster Box and pour out your love on Jesus.

Commit thy way unto the LORD; trust also in him;
and he shall bring it to pass.
Psalm 37:5

****

The rays of the sun, rising over the horizon, fell softly on her face.
It was the start of a new day.
She lifted her prayer to the Lord as she arose.
Quietly, purposely, she gathered the linen packet,
Its fragrance followed her steps
Up to the roof top,
In the sacred moments of silence
She would find there.
Sitting in the stillness, the colors of sunlight highlighting her hair,
She opened the folds of linen,
To reveal its contents.
The broken pieces of the Alabaster Box.
She lifted out one jagged piece and held it out
So the light would be reflected
In the beauty of the stone.
Holding that piece cupped in her hands,
She prayed.

Lord, I give You my all today.
Last night all I had to give was this box
And the ointment within.
But You knew what I was really giving,
I was giving my heart.
Today, the pieces may be broken,
But they still shine.
The oil may be spent,
But its fragrance remains.
Lord, Let Your beauty shine through me today.
Let each piece of my life
Radiate the wholeness
Only found in You.
She replaced the alabaster piece into the linen folds,
And arose.

Days, months, years had passed.
The linen had been sewn into a packet,
Holding its treasure still.
The fragrance had faded, but softly remained
If the cloth was held closely in her hands.
But the memory of that time was clear and strong.
In the morning she prayed.
Lord, Ahead of time, You said I anointed You.
That time came all so soon.
The jagged pieces of thorns pierced Your head,
They sought to break You there,
But Your love held You firm.
Your power overcame their plans.
Your purpose was fulfilled.
Your blood was spilled out.
Salvation had the fragrance of death
That day.
In the tomb, they wrapped You in fine linen cloths,

Shut and sealed the door.
Your beauty seemed sealed in that stone tomb,
Like the ointment had been sealed
In my Alabaster Box.
But You could not be held captive there,
The seal was broken,
The stone rolled away,
And You arose!
The fragrance of Your love meets me every day!
It is the fragrance of eternal Life!
The beauty of Your light still shines for all to see,
If they will but open their hearts to You.
Let the pieces of my life radiate Your love today,
Let Your fragrance follow my steps,
As I walk before others,
That they might know
You!
Lord, I pour out my devotion on You today,
Let my tomorrow be the same.
Anoint me with that hidden oil of blessing,
You will pour out on me.
I thank You, Lord, for that night,
So long ago,
When I could give You my all,
And You understood.
Thank You that You accepted the gift of my Alabaster Box.

Chapter Thirteen
Blessings

Take My Life, and Let It Be

Take my life, and let it be Consecrated, Lord, to Thee;
Take my hands, and let them move, At the impulse of Thy love,
At the impulse of Thy love.

Take my feet, and let them be Swift and beautiful for Thee;
Take my voice, and let me sing, Always, only, for my King,
Always, only, for my King.

Take my silver and my gold, Not a mite would I withhold;
Take my moments and my days, Let them flow in ceaseless praise,
Let them flow in ceaseless praise.

Take my will, and make it Thine, It shall be no longer mine;
Take my heart, it is Thine own, It shall be Thy royal throne,
It shall be Thy royal throne.

Frances R Havergal   *Caesar H. A. Malan*

****

Frances Havergal's hymn has stirred many hearts through the years. It is a song of dedication and commitment. It also is a summation of the journey of this book, Alabaster Boxes. Chapter Twelve seemed to be the closing thoughts for the study, yet as I sat quietly before the Lord, this beautiful hymn started to flow through my mind. I knew all the words by heart. It was one of the first Christian hymns I had memorized after being saved. The scope of dedication that the words spoke to my young heart years ago had brought tears to my eyes on first hearing it. I can remember being a young married woman and singing this song as I went about my house hold chores for the day. It became my hymn of prayer to my Lord.

So, it is this hymn that is to be added as a sonnet of praise and commitment to our study. Remembering that which we have learned and have been challenged by, let us take this hymn, one phrase at a time, as an appropriate summary to our time together. It would be so moving to stop at this point and just sing this song, "Take my Life, and Let it Be." Let us sing it together as an offering of praise to our Lord.

Personal Application:

Take my life, and let it be Consecrated, Lord, to Thee:
There is one highlighted word in this phrase. It is the word "consecrated." The Hebrew meaning of the word is that which is holy and set apart, counted as sacred. The English dictionary contains, in part, this definition: "Separating from the common to a sacred use, separating to the service and worship of God." What a glorious thought: my life, in all its commonness, can be separated for a sacred use in service and worship to my God! The same can be true for each of us. We are vessels made of clay, to be molded by the Potter's hands for His use. Oh, that God would consecrate each of our lives for His sacred service and worship.

What do you think is necessary for that consecration to take place in your life?

Joshua 6:19 has the command concerning the vessels for the LORD's house. *But all the silver, and gold, and vessels of brass and iron, are consecrated unto the LORD: they shall come into the treasury of the*

LORD. Note the word *"all"* and relate to the consecration of your life unto the Lord:

Read the following verses: Exodus 32:29, I Chronicles 29:5. Relate them to your own consecration:

Read Proverbs 23:26 and Romans 12:1. Note how consecration demands a voluntary giving of self to God:

Take my hands, and let them move, At the impulse of Thy love:
The concept of this phrase of the hymn is labor. We work with our hands. What a graceful picture there is in the imagery of the phrase. It is always beautiful to watch someone using Sign Language to communicate with someone else. To think that the use of our hands can communicate our devotion to God is a humbling thought.

According to the phrase, how are our hands to move?

Hands can be used to move in anger and hatred. How could a constant prayer about the use of our hands help in our lives?

What are some of the ways that the movements of our hands could convey God's love?

The Hebrew definition of the work "labor" is to serve and work for another. In this case that service is to be for God. The English dictionary defines labor as "persistent exertion." Note how important it is to remember the two words below in reference to the

labor of our hands:
        Service:

        Persistent:

II Chronicles 15:7: Be ye strong therefore, and let not your hands be weak: for your work shall be rewarded. Comment on the impact of this verse on consecration to God:

How are some of the ways that you could use your hands to work for the Lord?

Take my feet, and let them be Swift and beautiful for Thee:
        Feet are feet! No matter what definition. They are our means of transportation in most cases. Even if a person is handicapped and their feet cannot move them physically, there is always the desire to move forward in life. Our feet can take us many places. They can walk into dens of iniquity or into halls of praise, they can take us into deserted places of the world or into lecture rooms of learning, they can run from the place God would call us to or steadily move toward a place of witness. We may not think of our feet as beautiful, but many a tribe who was visited by a missionary who brought the news of salvation, would have thought that missionary's feet beautiful in purpose and direction! The places our feet take us, the messages they help us to carry, and the hurrying to aid someone in danger, make the decision concerning the Lord's guidance of our feet important.
        In David's prayer in II Samuel 22, he talks about his desire for the consecration of his own feet:
He [God] maketh my feet like hinds' feet: and setteth me upon my high places. Hinds are beautiful animals like the deer, or the mountain deer. In Biblical significance, they denote freedom,

steadiness, swiftness and grace. Comment on how II Samuel can apply to your life:

Think about the difference between stumbling with our own feet or walking on hinds' feet can be spiritually:

What kind of high places would David have desired for his life?

Read Psalm 40:2 and comment on the importance of stability for our feet on the Rock:

Read Isaiah 52:7 and comment on the meanings of "good tidings" and publishing "peace" can be to you as a Christian.

Write about the blessed meaning of the final phrase of the verse: *that publish salvation; that saith unto Zion, Thy God reigneth!*

In his commands for victorious Christian living, Paul wrote Ephesians 6:10-18. Note how the directions are given for the feet of a Christian:

How would this one verse's meaning help you to make wise decisions in life?

How can our witness be affected by where our feet take us?

Romans 10:8-15, is in a passage that speaks of how someone is truly saved and how the word of salvation comes to them. The last verse, Romans 10:15, echoes the words of the Old Testament we studied earlier, with a practical application. *And how shall they preach, except they be sent? as it is written, How beautiful are the feet of them that preach the gospel of peace, and bring glad tidings of good things!* What Christian responsibility and challenge do you find in that verse?

Take my voice, and let me sing, Always, only, for my King:
I love the adverbs, "always and only" in this verse. There is so much else we can use our voices for: rebuke, anger, useless discussions, criticism, songs of the world. But in our hymn, the desire is to sing always and only for my King.

Do you think that a person would have to just sing in church and from a hymnal to fulfill this desire?

If you are not gifted with a beautiful singing voice, can you still sing for God?

Note the importance that singing has in relationship to raising a baby:

Make a joyful noise unto the LORD, all ye lands.
Serve the LORD with gladness: come before his presence with singing.
Know ye that the LORD he is God: it is he that hath made us, and not we ourselves;

We are his people, and the sheep of his pasture.
Enter into his gates with thanksgiving, and into his courts with
praise:
Be thankful unto him, and bless his name.
For the LORD is good; his mercy is everlasting;
And his truth endureth to all generations.
Psalm 100

Read this beautiful Psalm several times and comment on its ministry
to your heart:

One of the Hebrew meanings for "sing" is to make a ringing
cry and shout for joy. David was also known as the "sweet psalmist"
of Israel. In fact, at the time of the approaching of his death, it is the
title the Lord gave to him. The English dictionary definition of
singing is to utter sweet sounds. The word "sweet" is used often
when speaking of the proper offerings to be given to the Lord. They
are to be of a sweet savour unto God. We should think of the offering
of our voice in praise as being of a sweet savour to our God, one that
brings Him pleasure. In Song of Solomon 2:14, the Rose of Sharon,
the Beloved champion, speaks of the one He loves, in representing
the Redeemed Bride of Christ. With tender love, He speaks: *O my*
dove, that art in the clefts of the rock, in the secret places of the
stairs, let me see thy countenance, let me hear they voice; for sweet
is thy voice, and thy countenance is comely.

Dear Lord, Lover of my soul,
Help my voice ever be sweet to Thy hearing.
Take from me any coarseness, or cruelty, anger or defense
and let it be all be sweet.
How blessed it is to my heart to know
that You hear my voice as sweet,
When it speaks to You of love,
when it sings of Your praises before men.

Take my voice, and let it sing,
Always, only for You, my King.

Take my silver and my gold, Not a mite would I withhold:

Many of us may not have any silver or gold, literally, but we all have things of value. Even if it is just a "mite," a small monetary unit. When I was a child, I can remember that in Missouri there were coins of smaller worth than a penny. They were called mills. They were not even made of valuable ore. Some were dyed red and made of plastic. But even a mill was based on the value of something greater. All around us we have possessions that have a monetary worth. Whether large or small, new or old, our homes have a value in money. They can be bought or sold. Commerce is a way of life. Whether it is a barter system in an old town market, a cash transaction or trading in stocks and bonds, there are money transactions all around the world. Conquests have been made for just one thing, the possession of silver and gold. Those two ores can be made into things of beauty like a sculptured necklace. They can purchase life-saving medications and items that are necessary to human comfort. But they can also be an allure that blinds some to anything but avarice, greed and manipulation. The challenge of our hymn is whether we can give our silver and gold to God with a willing heart. To place our possessions, fortunes and salaries into God's hands, not a mite withholding, is to ask His guidance as to the way that we would use it.

Things of value are not inherently evil. It is the way that we use them that actually determines their worth. Whether for destruction, ruin, growth or honor, the choice is ours to make.

Read and comment on the following verses concerning the misuse of monetary worth and their effect on men:

Proverbs 15:27:

Ecclesiastes 5:10:

I Timothy 6:10:
Contrast those negative verses with the following verses:

I Chronicles 29:9:

Proverbs 3:9:

What are some of God's guidelines for giving of our substance unto holiness?

II Corinthians 9:7:

II Corinthians 8:12:

Deuteronomy 16:17:

There is a mighty principle in the concept of giving all we have to the Lord. When we consider our possessions as belonging to God, we become accountable stewards of that wealth. Our accountability is to God who knows all and sees all. God is also the rewarder of those that are faithful and good stewards of money and possessions. The reward might be in peace instead of turmoil. Those that are greedy and always wanting more, are often depicted as striving in an almost vicious disregard for others. How sad that striving is. It brings an emptiness and lack of fulfillment, for there seems to never be enough gain. Yet when we give God control of this area of our lives, there is peace within. God knows our needs and He loves His children. We can trust Him to lead us aright. We might never be wealthy, but there will be a richness of peace within to replace striving. Our fulfillment is in Christ! When we have that commitment, then each dollar we gain is viewed with the joy of seeing how God will lead us to use it.

Oh Lord,
Not a mite would I withhold of that which You have given to me.
It is Yours already and now I pray it will be Yours doubly as I offer it
to You.
I do not want to be consumed by anything except the love and service
of Christ.
I want to be used.
If part of that using is found in my possessions, so be it.
Not a mite would I withhold.
If part of that using is in gaining so I can do more, so be it.
Not a mite would I withhold.
For You have given all for me.

Spiritual giving can be viewed as presenting something as a sacrifice and as a gift to God. It is even defined as yielding our rights over something to another. If our "Other" is Christ, than we can be motivated to give our all, even of our silver and our gold.

Give unto the LORD the glory due unto his name:
Bring an offering, and come into his courts.
Psalm 96:8

Take my moments and my days, Let them flow in ceaseless praise:

This phrase of the song presented two meditations: Our Moments and our Praise. Somehow, they seem to flow together in thought. What do we use our time for? Can we look back at the moments just prior in our hourly time march and know that with those moments, praise was brought to God by our lives? We do not have to stand on a corner and sing praises to God all day for our moments to show forth praise. Praise can be found in the gentle use of time to comfort a child, to create something beautiful for a loved one, to give testimony to someone who is crushed with life's burdens, to clean our homes so they shine for our Beloved Guest, Jesus. Praise is found in our moments or they are void of meaning. If we wake each morning and give that day to the Lord, it will be a glorious transformation of life. Wasted moments will vanish and be replaced by thoughtful moments. Time ill spent will become time treasured. Could it be that *my moments and my days* could actually *flow in ceaseless praise*? It can only happen when we give our time to God and our hearts to praise.

Sometimes just sitting by a river as the stream cools our weary feet is time we can spend resting in God. Those passing by might not see it, but God does. Sometimes lying in bed during sickness and taking the time to pray will bring peaceful praise. Even stirring a cake batter can be a time of quiet meditation on the love of family, praising God for each member. I have often rejoiced in times in the garden, even just pulling the weeds or pruning the roses. It seems to give me a quiet apartness to God. The noise and hustle of the world seems to fade away and I am softly brought into God's presence in just being with Him. We do not always have to be "doing" to allow our hearts to "be" in that place of praise.

Do you have peace today with your moments? It took a long time for me, a natural "doer", to learn the peace of just being in His presence in my moments. I am a list maker, and now I know that often my list is laid aside for countless moments when God will redirect my desire to complete, with His desire to complete my day with His purpose. The growth in my life has been to cease from trying to cram each hour with activity and fill each moment with Christ. Only then do I have peace. It can be that there will be much activity and work, or there will be quietness and rest. But I want it all to flow into endless praise.

Praise is defined in the English dictionary as homage offered as an act of worship and commendation. It also has the idea of giving thanks, lauding and confessing God. Following are verses with unique applications of the word Praise:

He is thy praise, and he is thy God. Deuteronomy 10:21. Praise here in the Hebrew contains the meaning of adoration. Write how this can affect the way you praise God.

Hear, O ye kings; give ear, O ye princes; I, even I, will sing unto the LORD; I will sing praise to the LORD God of Israel. Judges 5:3. Part of the Hebrew word for praise here is in blessing and kneeling before God. Write how this can affect the way you praise God.

And he appointed certain of the Levites to minister before the ark of the LORD, and to record, and to thank and praise the LORD God of Israel. 1 Chronicles 16:4. Here the word praise includes the concepts of boasting and shining forth concerning God. What are we to boast of in praise? How can you incorporate this into your praise of God?

And when he had consulted with the people, he appointed singers unto the LORD, and that should praise the beauty of holiness, as they went out before the army, and to say, Praise the LORD; for his mercy endureth for ever. II Chronicles 20:21. The second word for praise in this verse means to confess and to give thanks! How can you use this concept in your praise of God?

I will praise the LORD according to his righteousness: and will sing praise to the name of the LORD most high. Psalm 7:17. The two words for praise in this verse are from different Hebrew roots. The first means to laud, or give high honor to, and the second is simply to sing forth. What do these two meanings speak to your heart about?

Let the people <u>praise</u> thee, O God; let all the people praise thee. Psalm 67:3. Literally this word praise contains the idea of confessing the name of God! Relate this to your praise of God.

There are so many more verses with deep meanings of the word "praise" to be found in the Bible. Search out some today and claim one verse to memorize and make a part of your moments.

Take my will, and make it Thine, It shall be no longer mine:
One of the unique elements of God's creation of man is that He gave man a free will. We often think of this as simply the right to choose. The English dictionary describes *will* as the faculty or power of consciousness that allows deliberate action. That definition carries with it a tremendous responsibility. The choice is ours to do that which is pleasing to God or that which is contrary to His will. Adam and Even failed in the Garden of Eden in their choices. They had clear commandment from God not to eat of the fruit of the Tree of the Knowledge of Good and Evil and yet with deliberate action, they did. Sometimes, the choices of the exercise of our will are found to be dramatically clear cut. We can view the right or the wrong choice as if a shining light directed our thoughts. That Light should be of the Lord, if we have given Him our will, the instrument of choice. But if we are not strong in the power of God's might and in the study of His Word, the shining may be a deception, as it seems to have been for Eve. She was deceived in the Fall. Suddenly the fruit on the tree looked more beautiful and more desirable than that on any other tree around. Yet God had declared in His Creation that in Eden: *And the LORD God planted a garden eastward in Eden; and there he put the man whom he had formed. And out of the ground made the LORD God to grow every tree that is pleasant to the sight, and good for food... Genesis 2:8-9* God had provided that which was of good for Adam and Eve, the choice should have been clear, but they chose

incorrectly and failed. Every day choices have to be made in our lives. Some seem so simple as to be habitual. What outfit do we choose to wear, how to we style our hair, what food do we eat? Yet even in the "ordinary" there is choice. Is the outfit proper for the occasion? Is the hair style complimentary and clean? Is the food healthful and in proper portions?

The will is exercised all the day long. The results of the use of our will is to be of enormous impact on our tomorrows. That is why we need to give of our will to God. We need holy enabling, godly direction and Holy Spirit commitment to make the right choices, moment by moment. We have given God our time, now we need to give Him our will. Notice the song writer's word choice in this phrase. She writes: *Take my will, and make it Thine, It shall be no longer mine.* She uses such a strong word in "Take." It is as if she is realizing that in ourselves we cannot choose to even give over that will. After all, it is what sets us apart from the animals. It is "My Will," our pride says. Oh, but my will might choose incorrectly, it might see that shining fruit on the tree and ignore all the warnings, all the fragrant beauty of other fruit trees, all the consequences. Take it, Lord, take my will. I do not even trust myself to totally give it, but I am willing for You to reach into my sheltered self and take it! Then You can make it wholly, completely Thine!

Oh Lord,
That my will would move at Your command,
That my choice would be as You demand,
That my hand would reach out for Your best,
Only then can my soul have spiritual rest.

Yes, the need to have our will swallowed up in the will of God is a tremendous factor in spiritual growth and in the destiny of our tomorrows.

Note some verses of choice in the Scripture and comment on how they relate to your life:

Then Moses stood in the gate of the camp, and said, Who is on the LORD's side? Let him come... Exodus 32:26

I call heaven and earth to record this day against you, that I have set before you life and death, blessing and cursing: therefore choose life, that both thou and thy seed may live. Deuteronomy 30:19

Now therefore fear the LORD, and serve him in sincerity and in truth: and put ye away the gods which your fathers served on the other side of the flood, and in Egypt; and serve ye the LORD. And if it seem evil unto you to serve the LORD, choose you this day whom ye will serve; whether the gods which your fathers served that were on the other side of the flood, or the gods of the Amorites, in whose lands ye dwell: but as for me and my house, we will serve the LORD. Joshua 24:14-15

And Elijah came unto all the people, and said, How long halt ye between two opinions? If the LORD be God, follow him: but if Baal, follow him... I Kings 18:21

Then Jesus beholding him loved him, and said unto him, One thing thou lackest: go thy way, sell whatsoever thou hast, and give it to the poor, and thou shalt have treasure in heaven: and come, take up the cross and follow me. Mark 10:21

There are some beautiful verses that relate to the ultimate choice we have to follow God. In these verses, God is speaking to our hearts to make a decision of the will:

Come now, and let us reason together, saith the LORD: though your sins be as scarlet, they shall be as white as snow... Isaiah 1:18

Ho, every one that thirsteth, come ye to the waters... Isaiah 55:1

Come unto me all ye that labor and are heavy laden, and I will give you rest. Matthew 11:28

And the Spirit and the bride say, Come. And let him that heareth say, Come. And let him that is athirst come. And whosoever will, let him take the water of life freely. Revelation 22:17

What beauty there is in the call of God to our hearts to use our will to choose Him! In salvation, we will find life. In forgiveness, we will have release. In obedience, we will have victory. God's choices are for our good and for our growth. If you have not made the ultimate choice to come to God in salvation, believing His Word, trusting Him for the security of your soul, and believing in the redemption won by Christ on Calvary, make the decision today to simply and completely, Come.

Take my heart, it is Thine own, It shall be Thy royal throne:
It is a marvelous thing that God uses the term "heart" to speak of that which is vital to be given to the Lord. The hymnist sings, *Take my heart, it is Thine own, It shall be Thy royal throne.* Her heart was already God's! In deep devotion and complete trust, she had given her heart to God. Yet perhaps there was that one part, the part only she and God knew of, that needed to be totally given over to the Lord. It is as if she says, "Take it! I abdicate my desires and rights to sit on my own heart's throne, I want You to have it, Lord." Even when we are saved, redeemed, become God's child and asked Him into our hearts, there may be that part we strive to keep for ourselves. The English dictionary defines this use of the word "heart" as the seat of emotions, affections and passions. I wonder what emotion each of us wants to hang onto? Is it self-justified anger? Is it love of something not fit for God's service? What affections do we want to hang on to? Is it even the love of self and

the pride that comes with it? Is it love of another above what we should have for God? There is danger in that! What passions well up in our hearts when our emotions are stirred? Are they passions of love and commitment to God, or something else? Something we might think to justify because we are swayed by our passions?

No, Lord, let me not be half-hearted in following You.
Take all of my heart.
Then my emotions, my affections and passions
Will come from You.
They will be sweet with the fragrance of peace.
They will be crowned with the power of victory.
They will be becoming a servant of the Most High God,
Because my heart will be Thy Throne.
Rule there in all Your grace and majesty.
I humbly bow before Thee,
O Ruler of my Heart.

One of the kings of Israel that sought to bring back the people to God was Asa. In II Chronicles 15, we find that he was with the Lord, seeking Him with his own heart. Asa was strong and took courage to renew the commitment of his land to the true worship of God. He challenged the people of Judah to enter into a covenant to seek the LORD God with all their hearts and souls. They came together in a great assembly to so sware. *And all Judah rejoiced at the oath: for they had sworn with all their heart, and sought him [God] with their whole desire: .... The heart of Asa was perfect all his days. II Chronicles 15:15,17.* It is also interesting to note, that as long as Asa followed the Lord with all his heart, *there was no more war. II Chronicles 15:19.* Think of it, peace was a result of whole hearted commitment to God. Peace is what most of us long for in our lives. God's reign in our hearts brings in a realm of peace that overflows and saturates the soil prepared for growth in our lives. God sitting on the throne of our hearts is the only way we can be totally directed to be the servant, the follower, the steward of His reign.

In II Chronicles 15:17, Asa's heart is noted as being *perfect all his days*. How does that challenge your life today?

What do you think the word *perfect* means in that verse?

How did the spiritual decision Asa make in his own heart affect those around him?

Another concept of a spiritual heart is tied to the working of our conscience.
I Timothy 1:5 declares: *Now the end of the commandment is charity out of a pure heart, and of a good conscience, and of faith unfeigned.* Remembering that *charity* means godly love and *unfeigned* means sincere and without hypocrisy, write down what you feel this commandment means to your life:

Give your definition of the following from the verse:
    A pure heart:

    A good conscience:

    Faith unfeigned:

In the concordance of my Bible, "heart" was found under the heading of "Earnestness or Indifference." What a dynamic way of thinking of the working of our spiritual hearts! We can be earnestly committed and serving the Lord or completely indifferent. The choice is ours, but the difference in results are not only to ourselves, but far reaching as we saw with Asa. Following are some of the verses related to God's desire for our hearts:

And thou shalt love the LORD thy God with all thy heart, and with all thy soul, and with all thy might. Deuteronomy 6:5

Blessed are they that keep his testimonies, and that seek him with the whole heart. Psalm 119:2

Trust in the LORD with all thine heart; and lean not unto thine own understanding. Proverbs 3:5

And ye shall seek me, and find me, when ye shall search for me with all your heart. Jeremiah 29:13

God wants our hearts to be totally His. Every part. Every desire. Every passion. If we give Him all of our heart, then we will find that those things that we cherish in this world will be made more precious, the people we love will be held in closer, our goals will be directed in paths of shining Light.

Just as Mary poured out all of the ointment in that vessel of Alabaster, so our hearts should beat every moment for our Lord. What peace, what joy there is in loving the Lord with all our heart.

Oh Lord,
Take my heart and truly let it be not only Your dwelling place,
But a throne room of honor,
A place where I can feel Your presence,
And hear Your commands,
And listen to Your Words of counsel.
Let me sit at Your feet,
As my heart is drawn closer and closer to You.
Let me pour out all of myself,
Just as did the woman with the Alabaster Box.

****

Keep thy heart with all diligence; for out of it are the issues of life.
Proverbs 4:23
****

Quietly, thoughtfully Mary sat in the inner courtyard,
On the ledge of the pool of water,
That reflected the early morning rays
And colors of the sunrise.
She dipped her hands into the cool clear water,
Causing ripples to wash across the surface,
And spread the colors in patterns
Of serene beauty.
It was the dawn of the first day of the week.
How she remembered that Resurrection day so long ago.
Its light had seemed so strong even in Bethany.
Miles from Jerusalem,
Miles from where He had risen.
It was as if they had known the victory before the messenger came.
With the news,
He had Risen as He said!

Mary softly smiled. The ripples of color delighted her heart.
But she arose as it was that special day,
The day when others gathered in this place,
Gathered to worship her Lord,
Their Lord,
On the first day of the week.
Lazarus had said, there would be a letter from Paul,
Reminding them to live the Resurrection life,
Because He had risen as He said!
What joy that would be.

She drew her fingers one more time through the water,
    And thought,
            Lord, You caused the ripples of Your love
                To spread throughout Jerusalem
                And into this place in Judah,
                And way beyond.
        She had heard it reported and knew it was true.
What beauty there was in the ripples of His love,
What power there was in His promise,
        He had died, He had been buried and He had risen
            as He said!
New life He had come to bring, and He always kept His promises.

The years had gone by, but the promises were still true.
    Just as they had been when she sat at His feet,
    Just as they had been when she had poured out the ointment.
    Just as they had been when He had risen from the dead.
Quietly, softly Mary walked to her room and smelled the fragrance.
    It was still there after all this time,
            Not as strong now,
            But just as real.
    Thank You Lord,
            For allowing me to break the Alabaster Box,
            And pour out the ointment on You.
            And for accepting my gift of love,
                As small as it was.
    Thank You Lord,
            For hanging on the Cross for sin's payment,
            For enduring the pain,
            And pushing aside the darkness of the tomb.
    Thank You Lord,
            For rising again and shouting to my heart,
                It is finished,

The victory is won.
Thank You Lord,
That You live still in Glory above.
And one day I will see You there.
In my first day of timeless eternity.
Help me to share that with others today,
So they, too, can pour out their love,
At Your blessed nail pierced feet.
That were covered with precious ointment,
That night so long ago.

****

Be ye therefore followers of God as dear children;
And walk in love, as Christ also hath loved us,
and hath given himself for us an offering and a sacrifice to God
for a sweet-smelling savour.
Ephesians 5:1-2

Dedication

There were several women I approached asking if I would have their permission to dedicate this book to them. Each one declined. Perhaps it was humility, perhaps privacy, but they did not feel they should be that one to fit the purpose of the book. Then as I prayed, I realized that there were many women I know who have "done what they could" for the Lord. What a blessing! Some have been missionaries: several carried on the work alone, some faced death, several others had their ministry changed by different situations and yet found broader ministries God had prepared for them. Their common denominator: faithfulness. To them I dedicate this book. God knows who you are.

Then there are the women in unique Christian service who have "done what they could" often because of the physical and health situations of their lives. One, a dear friend and witness to my husband as a young man, was stricken by severe arthritis, yet continued serving even from her hospital bed. Another, a brilliant young Christian lady of severe disabilities, who has used those disabilities and her diligence to create programs for others and to always witness for Christ. God gave them unique ministries. Their common denominator: indomitable spirit. God knows who you are.

Then there are the women, others might not consider in "full time service," yet they are servants in their lives. Stay at home moms, teachers, pastors' wives, neighbors and friends. There are special ones I can call to mind that have truly "done what they could" in the place God ordained for them. They may not think their scope of influence is great, but the ripples of the circles of their ministries will ever widen. God chose each of them for their special service. Their common denominator: grace dispensers. God knows who you are.

Perhaps you, dear reader, know someone in your life that has ministered uniquely to you. They have "done what they could" to be witnesses for Christ and for His Kingdom. That gentle word, that personal touch or deed of kindness, often going beyond the "norm" of everyday living. Their common denominator: love of Christ and of others. God knows who they are, too.

Each of us has the opportunity to be faithful women of indomitable spirit, who are grace dispensers through the love of Christ and others. We, too, can have this phrase applied to our lives: "they have done what they could." Let each of us strive to give of ourselves for God's glorious service. The dedication of the Biblical concepts of this study can be ours as we remain truly committed to the Lord. Never lose hope, God knows who each of us is!

About the Author:

Barbara Ellen Houston McCain and her husband, Dennis have been in the ministry for over forty years. Dennis was in the pastorate and evangelism, and they together served as missionaries for thirty-three years. At the present time they are retired, but still serving in support ministries and Barbara in writing. They have three grown and married children, plus grandchildren and great grandchildren.

It is the author's burden to share with others the love of the Scriptures and the joy of life found in the Lord Jesus Christ. Since retirement, she has started recording book ideas that have filled a special place in her heart for this purpose. At the time of the publishing of this book, *Alabaster Boxes*, there are other women's Bible studies, and also Christian fiction, by this author available on line. A list of these will follow. It is the author's prayer and burden that each of her books will challenge ladies of today to treasure the gift of the lessons from the Bible in their lives and understand the wonderful privilege it is to know Jesus Christ as their personal Savior.

The author's life verse is also her prayer for those that join in her circle of readers:

That ye might walk worthy of the Lord unto all pleasing,
Being fruitful in every good work,
And increasing in the knowledge of God;
Colossians 1:10

Women's Bible Studies and Devotionals

Lessons From Ladies of Faith
> *Studies in the lives of select women in the Bible that teach us lessons of the life of faith for us today.*

The Not So Minor Prophets
> *Major lessons for Women from the Minor Prophets*

Women's Christian Fiction

The Elizabeth Series:
> *Wind, Sea, and Skye*
> > *A Step Journey of Faith*

> *Owl's Bend*
> > *Part One: Well Watered Meadow*

All these books and *Alabaster Boxes* can be found at Amazon.com and Kindle e-books. It is the author's prayer that more books will be added to the list and can be found by searching her author's name: Barbara Ellen Houston McCain.